# ABBEY LEIX AI

## O'MORE ARTICLES ON THE ART AND DESIGN OF EDUCATION

### VOLUME THREE

ABBEY LEIX ANTHOLOGY
Copyright © 2012 by O'More College of Design
ISBN-10: 0-9846244-8-1
ISBN-13: 978-0-9846244-8-5

Portions edited by Rosemary Hilliard,
Ashley Balding, and Jessa R. Sexton
Illustrations by Sarah Keaggy
Cover photography by Jessa R. Sexton
Back cover photography by Malerie Serley
Cover design by Courtney Allen and Sarah Keaggy
Interior layout by Courtney Allen and Sarah Keaggy

Published by:
O'More Publishing
A Division of O'More College of Design
423 South Margin St.
Franklin, TN 37064 U.S.A.

# ABBEY LEIX ANTHOLOGY

O'MORE ARTICLES ON THE ART AND DESIGN OF EDUCATION

VOLUME THREE

O'MORE
PUBLISHING

FRANKLIN, TENNESSEE

## MEANINGFUL EXPRESSION
By Eloise Pitts O'More

The following are excerpts from two letters from the founder and first president of O'More College of Design: Mrs. Eloise Pitts O'More. Her passion for design, for looking at the technical as well as the inner spirit of things, is evident in her writings. The letters had much overlap in exact wording and content, though one was written "to colleges and friends" January of 1993 and the other later that year to faculty. The intent of her writing was not changed, but the letters were merged here in hopes you would read all of her words without skipping the second letter because of its redundancy.

I was fortunate enough to meet Mrs. O'More before I graduated high school more than ten years ago. If you were not so privileged, I am sure you know her anyway. Her vision and legacy are obvious all around us; I feel certain she would be proud of O'More as it stands today. After you read this letter, I think you'll start seeing her everywhere: not just in the paintings of her in the library and Abbey Leix Mansion parlor, but in the energy and excitement of our faculty, in the courtesy and cleverness of our staff, in the drive and direction of our curriculum, and in the interest and intensity of your own heart.

Jessa R. Sexton
Executive Editor, O'More Publishing
Associate Professor, Liberal Arts

---

I look forward to the Faculty Meeting in August. It will offer the pleasant opportunity of greeting those who are returning as well as becoming better acquainted with the teachers who are joining O'More for the first time.

Even though having recently relinquished a portion of my usual duties with O'More College, I assure you that my initial interest and concern for the excellence and the progress of the college still prevails. In fact, the mounting scale of this era's materialistic thinking has alerted me to re-emphasize O'More's original "Reasons for Being."

As all of you know this college was founded on the ideal of nurturing and enriching human existence both through external environment and the profound wisdom of the inward spirit...thus recognizing each student as unique and very special, worthy of the most careful guidance, example, and challenge.

The implications of this philosophy go far beyond the catalog-stated curriculum. From it's origin I have never envisioned this school as solely concerned with the facts, skills, and practice of a profession. My conception of teaching design includes those illusive, yet most compelling qualities, too, difficult to encompass with words. It has to do with the eternal yearning of humanity for a <u>meaningful expression</u>. As plants on earth ever turn toward the sun for growth and strength, so also the human spirit instinctively leans toward an inward harmony ever longing to capture its reflection through some mode of accomplishment.

All persons involved in an art-related study should frequently be encouraged to pause and become aware of the inner wisdom since we ask our students to create through both inward and outward faculties. Skills are necessary for adequate visual statements, yet if the inner vision does not burn brightly through the finished effort, the expression will contain no pulse of life. It will not satisfy the student, neither will it excite or convince the world.

Objectivity of vision is an integral part of the creative process. Unfortunately few people seem to realize this; mainly, I suspect, because it is not easily practiced.

Students in my class receive an enlightening example of viewing themselves with objectivity in their first assignment, even though at the time they are not aware of it.

The project: take a journey back into your early childhood home where you lived before your tenth birthday, sketch a floor plan of that structure, (mansion, cottage, apartment, mobile home) whatever it might have been. Present the sketch to the class, and take them on a tour through the house, describing every detail of furnishing and decorations as well as you can remember. Also include any emotional feelings about it, such as spaces you either loved or disliked or felt uncomfortable in. Describe the yard or grounds also, and tell us where you often played.

Naturally this experience evokes a multitude of memories, ...happy, sad, joyful, and sometimes very painful ones. I am forever surprised at the ease, the candor, the honesty of the students' responses. It is as if they were tracing the movements and thoughts of a person apart from themselves. It is a gratifying manifestation of objectivity. The students invariably tell me that they have gained from it.

Finally, let me repeat that I regard O'More's founding ideal, the idea, the dream as viable and enduring, in spite of the confusion and stress of changing times. It has been proven that institutions as well as human beings function with more enthusiasm and success when they are living out a dream.

At our meeting, let's discuss how we can keep this dream alive.

With this month O'More is beginning its twenty-fourth year. In looking back I am proud that we have more than four hundred graduates in the work-place who have received quality training. Many have accomplished outstanding work. And I am deeply grateful for our reputation for excellence. this fact has always renewed my spirit even on the most discouraging days.

Yet, today I find myself deeply concerned about our future in this world of traumatic change and brutally competitive attitudes. Never before have I been so fearful of decisions and plans. I have always pushed ahead believing I could make it work. Now it seems difficult to stand aside and view the school objectively.

Your objective view, your ideas, your suggestions are needed and will be deeply appreciated.

Sincerely,

Eloise O'More.

# TABLE OF CONTENTS

# TABLE OF CONTENTS

Ashley Balding is a fashion design student at O'More and journalist for O'More Publishing. She is a Nashville native and loves doing anything creative including writing, sewing, and painting. She also loves watching old movies, listening to music, and spending time with family.

# THE PLIGHT OF THE CURVY WOMAN

ASHLEY BALDING
*O'More Publishing Journalist*
*Student, Fashion*

FOR AT LEAST THE LAST DECADE, it seems to have become a trendy topic to talk about curvy women in the media. For generations we have been bombarded with idea of the perfect body and the perfect appearance. The Nineties gave us the starvation-style-Kate-Moss-esque, stick-thin models with bones poking through their paper-thin skin.

I have never been a stick. Even when I was little I had curves. Nobody ever made fun of me, but I always felt out of place. My legs were fleshy when other girls' were twig-like. I was wearing women's jeans in middle school, when the "cute" girls were still shopping at Limited Too. I remember in elementary school we had to gather in the cafeteria every morning. I would only sit in one certain position (on my knees with a jacket sitting on top of my legs) because I did not want anybody to think my legs looked fat.

Fat.

The big, bad F word. I hate that word. I despise it. Not just because we all feel it sometimes, but I hate the connotation. I hate the way it makes me feel. I hate how it eats away at you little by little until all that is left is an inhuman nub of negativity. And everybody deals with this.

Now when I look back at childhood pictures, I know that I was definitely nowhere near fat. I was simply normal. I wasted so much time worrying, even as a ten year old, about what people thought of me. And I know young girls do the same these days.

Thankfully, there is consistently more attention on the skinny girl image in the media. But my problem with that is I don't want someone in my magazine that is the token "plus-size girl" to represent my supposed normal size. I hate opening a magazine and seeing skinny girl, skinny girl, skinny girl, and then one huge girl, who looks even huger because she is plastered next to the skinny girls, with big red flags saying, "Look at me I'm plus-size! Give this magazine some credit!" That, to me, is worse than having all boney models. It's as if the magazines think that by simply including one big girl, it's going to appease all the women out there. WRONG!

The closest thing to "real" that I think I have seen thus far is the model Lizzie Miller, otherwise known as "the girl on page 194." Miller is considered a plus-size model, but looks nothing near overweight (at least to me). *Glamour* featured her in a 3x3 inch picture that took the world by storm when its September issue hit the stands last year. Miller has gone on to appear in more editorials and talk about her experiences on talk shows. Miller is a beautiful woman who truly represents a normal physique—one that we can all attain.

What I don't get is that she is called plus-size. If there is one term that I hate more than "fat" it is "plus-size." Who decided that plus-size would be a great way to describe women? Last time I checked plus-size wasn't the same type of compliment as "you are stunning." That's not true in all cases, but I know that if a man (or woman) walked up to me and said, "Wow, you are plus-size!" I would NOT take it as a compliment. It has a negative connotation to it, and I really don't believe that we need to attach that term to ourselves.

Whatever happened to the days when a woman's curves were not just celebrated, but a normal characteristic, anyways? In the classical Greco-Roman age, women's bodies were depicted as round, muscular, fleshy, and curvy. This represented beauty, strength, and fertility—all things that women should be and are—the NORM.

As someone who hopes to one day make an impact in the fashion industry, I struggle with this concept of "normal" body types. When the media is so skinny-girl-laden, how are women supposed to even know what to put on their bodies? This is something that I think about every day that I get dressed. There are several celebrities out there who are curvy, womanly, and beautiful, and I often channel their style in moments of frustrated outfit contemplation.

Kate Winslet has always been one of my style icons. She is classy and beautiful in that understated, Old Hollywood kind of way. She is fierce and feminine, two qualities that I admire and desire to be a part of my persona. When I look at her style and how to translate it into my wardrobe there are a few key elements that can be incorporated:

- Stick with classic styles—cardigans, trouser pants, pencil skirts, tailored blazers. Feel free to play around with prints, patterns, and bold colors, but stick to simple styles that are structured in the right spots.
- Don't be afraid to stand out—speaking of prints, patterns, and bold colors: never be afraid to use them! The right print can fool the eye and make your body look flawless. Put bold colors on parts of your body that you want to draw the most attention to. If you love your legs, wear a tomato red pencil skirt. The eye will be directed toward your favorite spot.
- A little sex appeal never hurt anybody—be proud of your body. Kate is a pro at showing a little bit of skin, but not too much. It's usually just enough to give off an air of sex appeal.
- When in doubt, throw a little retro in—Kate embodies that Old Hollywood, glamorous feel. Vintage styles encourage a curvy figure and are always a win in my book. Try wearing a full skirt with a wide belt and a fitted top. Be sure to always show off the smallest part of your waist. Proportions are everything!
- Red lips can save you—there are some days when nothing feels right, and you just can't get your fashion mojo to line up, with or without Kate's help. On days like this red lips can give you just enough oomph to make you feel sexy, classy, and lady-like. Kate does this perfectly all the time.

These are just a few tips to get you going on those mornings that you're standing in front of your closet, without a clue as to where to start. I know I find myself in that spot far too often. Remember that no matter what, love the skin you're in, and dress accordingly. There are so many women out there to look up to, whether the fashion industry is promoting it or not. As fellow females, we need to combine forces and be proud of who we are. It's time for a beauty revolution, and it can start with our choices standing in front of that closet every morning!

Lori Bumgarner is O'More College of Design's Fall 2011 Artist-in-Residence. She is an image consultant and owner of paNASH Style where she specializes in wardrobe styling, media coaching, and career coaching. She received a Bachelor of Arts from the University of North Carolina, Charlotte, and Master of Education from the University of South Carolina. Bumgarner recently penned *Advance Your Image* and is an Amazon #1 Bestselling Author.

# FASHION WORTH HANGING ONTO

LORI BUMGARNER
*Owner, paNASH Style*

I ONLY MAKE IT to the Frist Center for the Visual Arts on few occasions, usually when family or friends are visiting. However, on my last visit there a little over a year ago, I went alone to see the popular exhibit *The Golden Age of Couture (Paris and London, 1947-1957),* which I was excited to see given my love for both fashion and history. When I returned home from the museum that day, I became my own little curator of historical fashion artifacts.

Two weeks prior to my visit to the Frist, I had traveled back home to North Carolina where I finally picked up a box of keepsakes my sister had been storing for me ever since I first made the move to Nashville five years ago. And for those entire two weeks I had been driving around with that box in the back of my SUV. After seeing the exhibit at the museum that day I finally decided to go ahead and try to lift the heavy box of memories out of my car.

Since it had been so long since I last went through the box, I couldn't recall exactly all that was in it. There were a few items I remembered and expected to see when I opened the box, but there were at least three items I had recently been wondering, "Whatever happened to that?" (Is that a coincidence? Probably not since I don't believe things are just coincidences.) Finally, I found some things that I had completely forgotten were in there, some "historical fashion artifacts" that I'm sure will never end up on display at the Frist but are just as priceless to me.

Now as both a woman and a wardrobe stylist, you can be certain that I possess a healthy (or perhaps unhealthy) love for shoes. Well, while searching through my keepsakes, I found one of my first pairs of baby shoes. (See picture.) Of course this first pair of shoes were flats, but seeing these made me remember getting my first pair of high heels when

I was in only the 2nd grade…they were a pair of Candies for little girls, during the time when Candies first became really popular. (Yes, it was the early '80s.) I wasn't supposed to wear them to school, but I begged my mom to let me even though they made my feet hurt something fierce. I guess my mom understood the universal female truth that sometimes style takes precedent over comfort, and so she let me don them one day to school. I don't quite know why I felt the need to be styling in high heels in the 2nd grade.

Speaking of my mother and shoes, I also found in the keepsake box a pair of my mom's shoes I had kept when we went through her personal belongings right after her death from cancer over ten years ago. They were the pair of shoes that went with the dress she was buried in. At this point you may be wondering why was she not buried in those shoes along with the dress. Proof that you learn something new every day, the funeral home told us that it was unnecessary to include her shoes in her final dressing since nobody sees that part of the body during the viewing anyway. So, I kept them as a reminder of the bittersweet time spent with my mother as she planned the details of her own funeral. She had asked me to be the one to choose the outfit for her to be buried in. (Mind you, this was long before I became a wardrobe stylist.) I chose a dress that was her favorite color, pink. It was one that she had previously worn on two very special occasions: my sister's wedding and my debutante ball. My mother always looked beautiful in this dress, and even though it had become too big for her due to the weight loss from her illness, the funeral home used their tricks of the trade to make it look perfect on her.

In addition to mine and my mother's shoes, I also found among my memories my very first skirt (a tiny red skirt with three white buttons that probably fit me when I was only about one or two years old) and several pairs of adult-sized satin white gloves. I think some of the gloves were ones my mother wore with her gowns when she attended the annual Marine Corps ball with my father, and a couple of pairs belonged to me including a pair I wore to prom and an over-the-elbow pair I had to have for my deb ball. Seeing all the couture clothing and photographs at *The Golden Age of Couture* exhibit and then finding those gloves made me wish I lived in a time of such elegance. But then seeing in the art display all the torture-device-type undergarments women had to wear in the 40s and 50s made me thankful I live in this century!

Probably the funniest items I found in the keepsake box were my old Barbie dolls dressed in my favorite outfits I had picked out for them, along with one of the fashion plates from my Tomy Toys Fashion Plates that my grandmother had given me for Christmas one year. (See picture.)

Because of all the hours I would spend dressing my Barbies and creating designs from my Fashion Plates, I knew I wanted to one day work in fashion. It took me a while to get there because first I had to (with much trial and error) develop my own sense of style, but there were also other things I had to learn that would prepare me for working with such unique clients as recording artists.

Some people may look at clothes, shoes, and other fashion artifacts as just material things, and in the grand scheme of it all, they are just that, things. But like numerous other objects such as an old guitar or an antique fountain pen, fashion artifacts can inspire creativity and even a purposeful career. And they can hold sentimental value that invokes loving memories that are absolutely irreplaceable!

Nicole Flatt is finishing her final semester at O'More College of Design and will graduate in May from the Interior Design Department. This article is the first half of her final paper in Research and Documentation, a senior level course at O'More, and was nominated for publication in this anthology by her department chair.

# GUIDING PROGRESSION
## THROUGH ARCHITECTURAL AND DESIGN ELEMENTS

### NICOLE FLATT
*Student, Interior Design*

INTERIORS HOUSING UNWORTHY EXPERIENCES

"Architecture is produced by ordinary people, for ordinary people; therefore it should be easily comprehensible to all" (Rasmussen 14). However, "in modern cities throughout the world our sense of orientation, knowing where and who we are, is damagingly compromised. Offices, apartments, and stores are piled together in ways which owe more to filing-cabinet systems than to a concern for human existence or experience" (Bloomer 4).

"Greater environmental legibility facilitates greater exploration, which leads to greater understanding or at least to a sense of familiarity, all of which promotes greater overall satisfaction with an environment" (Kopec 91). When one approaches a building, a typical step process takes place including "approach, arrival, waiting, moving to destination place, arriving at the destination, performing the intended activity, taking side trips, engaging in peripheral activities, departing from the destination, moving toward the exit, and exiting" (Rengel 20-21). Each of these steps requires movement through the space. This proves how important it is for the user to be able to navigate through the space easily and without confusion, because "the ability to navigate through an environment easily influences our overall perception of it" (Kopec 91), and "it is far easier, simpler to create spaces that work for people than those that do not" (Whyte 348).

This information shows the importance of studying how people psychologically perceive and progress through spaces as well as the importance of using that found information to create spaces that are easily navigable. If interior designers design in a way that allows for understandable circulation or wayfinding, it would eliminate the need for excess signage, which eliminates the need to bring in an extra person (such as a graphic designer) to the design team. It would also eliminate the need for concierges or other related people who are paid to give direction. When asked how she felt about constantly being asked where the restrooms are in the restaurant she works at, Sierra Pena, waitress and hostess at O'Charleys, responded, "It is very distracting from my work to explain and sometimes to have to guide people to the restrooms." She later expressed her agreement that "if it can be done to design a space where people can navigates themselves around, it would be much more ideal" (Pena). Clear wayfinding leads to more efficiency, a pleased client, and more comfort for users of the space.

To incorporate this philosophy into designs, a designer can use certain elements that cause users of the building to progress through and interact with the spaces in the designers' desired way. One must keep in mind that "how we find our way in the world is a psychological process that can be highly subjective and individual" (Kopec 90). All people in the world are diverse—in their struggles, aspirations and dreams, careers, past experiences, likes or dislikes, and material preferences, among a million other things—resulting in each person interpreting things uniquely. The study of people's progression must be very in depth to make good use of it.

Therefore, the relevance of this inquiry is that a designer could take the psychological backgrounds of the proposed users of the specified space(s) and use this information to enhance how the space works for this specific group of people. "For if [users] cannot thrive in [the designer's] house its apparent beauty will be of no avail—without life it becomes a monstrosity" (Rasmussen 12). A space that no one can navigate or experience in a relevant way is of no function to society. A building that requires a multitude of signs, which take away from its aesthetics, and still cannot direct people in a simple way, is also of no use to society. Hence, designers and architects alike need to begin using the psychological aspects of how users interpret and move through spaces to create more thoughtful, navigable designs.

In order to further investigate this reasoning and to apply it to design, one could research how people interpret and move through spaces and go a step further and find out why they do this. One should achieve a discovery of what causes a person to move towards a yellow wall rapidly, or what the effect a large space has on circulation opposed to a small one. Researching how different architectural and design elements can cause different pushes and pulls will help one to better understand how to use these elements in a way that will allow for easier navigation of his designs.

*****

## PSYCHOLOGY OF DIFFERENCES IN PROGRESSION
## (WHY PEOPLE PROGRESS)

There can be many different reasons why people progress. One main aspect is sensory information. Sight, sound, smell, touch, and taste can all cause someone to move towards or away from an area. For example, "the way sound acts in an enormous cathedral, with its echoes and long-toned reverberations" could attract people towards that sound, "compared to a small paneled room, well-padded with hangings, rugs and cushions" where there would not be any sound produced to attract people (Rasmussen 33). "Every living thing on earth reacts to sensory stimulation" (Kopec 23). An important point of the senses related to progression is that of arousal. Arousal can result from one of the five senses and spark one's curiosity to learn more about what caused that particular sense to be aroused. However, designers must keep in mind that "each of our five senses can be overstimulated or understimulated," and he should strive for a mean of the two (Kopec 23). There should be just enough sensory information going on to keep one engaged, but not so much that people become overstimulated and can no longer effectively cope with the information.

"Cultures, traditions, and history also contribute to our preferences and perspectives of the world" (Kopec 81). All cultures possess different attributes related to color preferences, meanings of things, varied aesthetic preferences, etc. "That which may be quite right and natural in one cultural environment can easily be wrong in another; what is fitting and proper in one generation becomes ridiculous in the next when people have acquired new tastes and habits" (Rasmussen 10-11). These preferences would cause people from different cultural backgrounds to perceive architectural elements differently causing diverse ways of progression. This is also true for traditions and history, as well as what people call social norms. Each of these things can cause people to have different perceptions of anything they encounter.

Another point of perception involves scenographic and abstract representations. These are "ways in which people perceive, comprehend, and store information" (Kopec 90). Scenographic representations include picture-based information, and abstract representations are those of a data-based nature. People who prefer scenographic representation use things like landmarks or images to help them navigate spaces, whereas people who prefer an abstract method tend to pay more attention to actual mileage or street signs. There also exists a group of people who use a combination of both these methods. These are ways in which people progress through space by using personally understood methods that help them figure out where they are going. This can be helpful to navigation if a designer understands this concept and includes things such as landmarks, pictures, or other means to allow people to develop this better understanding of where they are.

A rather obvious reason for progression is someone having a planned destination. As previously mentioned, there is a typical step process that people go through when encountering a building; these steps speak a lot about how one will reach his planned destination. Understanding this process will help a designer to design his building in a way that allows people to reach their destinations easily.

In order to reach planned destinations, "[People] use cognitive maps as well as the physical objects and elements within a space to locate and reach [their] destination as efficiently as possible" (Kopec 91). "Research indicates that the number one method of wayfinding by humans is through the use of landmarks" (91). Designers could, therefore, add these aforementioned objects or landmarks to make it easier for people to navigate the given spaces. Designers should also look into the program for the design and determine what areas will be most commonly used and create easily understood navigation to these specific areas.

People also progress based on the concept of pushes and pulls, moving away from something unsettling behind them or moving toward something of interest ahead. One concept of this is related to "Serial Vision, which theorizes that urban scenes are experienced as a series of revelations, as current views juxtapose with emerging views" (Cullen

167). "A long straight road has little impact because the initial view is soon digested and becomes monotonous. The human mind reacts to a contrast, to the difference between things…Unless this happens the town will slip past us featureless and inert" (169). This contrast happens by considering "two elements: the existing view and the emerging view" (169). People experience spaces through revelations of each point they are coming to and leaving behind; making these points memorable will allow for better understood spaces.

People also make themselves part of the place they are in; they encounter things in a way that includes themselves in the space. Therefore, one should consider making the experience of progression one that people would enjoy being a part of, encouraging exploration. "To successfully navigate an environment—which changes constantly as we move through it—we must continually acquire, process, release, recall, and respond to different stimuli and objects" (Kopec 90). To further research progression, one should look at specific elements or objects that could be perceived differently and develop an understanding for how each of these given elements will cause general progression or experience through designed spaces.

*****

INTERPRETATION OF VARIOUS DESIGN ELEMENTS

There are several different elements in design that can be used to control how a user progresses through a space. These elements should be used in one's design in ways that cause movement toward the designated areas and away from areas that are off limits to users. If done properly, these elements can create a proposed environment that can be navigated with ease, with no need for a map or sign.

DECORATION ASPECTS: COLOR, LIGHTING, AND MATERIALS

*Color*

"People require varying, cycling stimuli to remain sensitive and alert to their environments" (Birren 38). This can easily be done in interior spaces through the use of color. "Wayfinding often makes use of color," and there are even set meanings for colors worldwide that could allow them to be used to affect progression (Kopec 90). To use colors as a way of increasing wayfinding abilities, one could place colors in areas that would affect how people then perceive and progress from or towards that area. "Warmness and high intensities are said to be usually active and stimulating, while cool hues and low intensities are more subdued and relaxing" (Ching, *Interior Design Illustrated* 114). This could be incorporated by creating a social area where one is supposed to arrive and stop for a while in a warmer hue, and somewhere that people should move away from could be cooler hues.

"Bright saturated colors and any strong contrasts attract our attention; grayed hues and middle values are less forceful" (Ching, *Interior Design Illustrated* 114). This information could also be applied by painting a room at the end of a passage a bright color or a group of contrasting colors to pull people that direction. Whereas, if there is an area the designer would like to keep certain users of the space away from, it could become a more grayed area and would be less noticeable to the public eye. It is also important for a designer to remember that "the warmth or coolness of a color's hue, along with its relative value and degree of saturation, determines the visual force with which it attracts [one's] attention" (Ching, *Interior Design Illustrated* 114). This concludes that not only bright colors can attract a user's attention, but even a dull color with high saturation or value level could be an attention grabber.

There are also, as said above, some general responses to certain colors. These colors can be used to achieve precise responses, but one must keep geographical location in mind because the same color can hold extremely diverse meanings in different locations. For example, the color orange in the United States is strongly associated with hazards or, on a psychological side, sociality, luminosity, or warmth; however, if one finds himself designing a building in Egypt, orange represents mourning in their culture and would be taken offensively if used in a space to inspire sociality. This is something to definitely keep in mind when using color to set a mood for some sort of progression tactic.

*Light*

"Light is the prime animator of interior space" (Ching, *Interior Design Illustrated* 126). All building interiors must include lighting; designers can use this area of a design to improve wayfinding as well.

Light can be of two forms: natural or artificial.

The most obvious examples of natural lighting include the sun and the moon. This type of lighting can be achieved through openings in the walls or ceiling of a space. Such lighting can be used for wayfinding in many different applications. One way it could pull people towards a space is if there exists a somewhat dark area with a glimpse of a room ahead that is very naturally lit and extremely bright. People are going to gravitate towards that area due to the contrast. There is also the application of one simple window "framed within a wall plane attract[ing] people's attention with [its] brightness and outlook" (Ching, *Interior Design Illustrated* 38).

Natural lighting also tends to be an attractor just because of its brightness. People enjoy sunbathing or even simply relaxing in natural light, which obviously means they are going to progress towards it. It is also important to have natural lighting in a building because it psychologically helps people to feel more energized and focused.

Artificial lighting is often used in spaces where there is no option to use natural lighting. It is also used as back up in areas with a lot of natural lighting, for times when nature simply is not producing sufficient light in that area. As with natural lighting, there are many application possibilities for artificial lighting as well. One potential use is that "local lighting can...partition a space into a number of areas" (Ching, *Interior Design Illustrated* 128). This could cause people to stop progression, not to pass through a specific point in the space, or to move along the 'light wall' that is created through this application. Later on there will be discussion of a segmentation bias in which people break large spaces up mentally to take them in with more ease, and this use of lighting would be an excellent way to aid in that process for oversized spaces. Lighting can also be used to create a path the designer wants people to take. For instance, if the designer wants people to travel diagonally through the middle of a space, he could place strip lights in the floor outlining this path, and it would definitely encourage people to stay on the path and gently push them along.

Another thing to understand is that it may not be lighting, but possibly the absence of lighting, that causes people to progress. A big part of studying progression is realizing people not only gravitate towards things but also move away from things as well. A bright light could pull people forward, while an uncomfortably dark space can easily push people away just as effectively. Simply put, there is a meaningful opportunity to create better flowing spaces by putting a little effort into the area of lighting design. "Whether natural or artificial, light accentuates objects or spaces, suggests movement and circulation[,] and aids the understanding of the interior of a building" (Brooker 160).

### Material Selection

One last area related to the 'decoration' of a space to aid in progression is that of material selection. As with other topics discussed in this section, contrast is a strong point when it comes to materials causing progression as well. For example, very soft, plush carpeting suddenly breaking into a cold, hard tiling is something that could put an immediate stop to progression. It could also be seen as simply a transition, which is showing the change of environments. It could be inviting to find out what the next environment is. This point is also stated in a quote from Bloomer: "Changes of texture often signal special events and can trigger a slowing or quickening of one's pace" (71). Another aspect of materials is that of smooth materials versus rough materials: "Smooth surfaces invite close contact, while rough materials such as hammered concrete generate movement in wide radii around corners and more careful, tentative movement through corridors" (Bloomer 71).

## ARCHITECTURAL 'LINES:' ANGLES, CURVES, AND STRAIGHTS

When thinking of progression, one generally imagines a path, whether defined conventionally or not. "All paths of movement...are linear in nature" (Ching, *Architecture* 264). The following three types of linear organization, angles, curves, and straights, can be used to define literal paths, but they could also be small hints in materials or overhead planes, furniture arrangements, or any other of a multitude of things. Each of these elements has an extremely strong influence on progression.

### Angles

The first of this grouping involves angles, which could also be called diagonals. "Diagonal lines...imply movement and are visually active and dynamic" (Ching, *Interior Design Illustrated* 95). The importance of stimulation in ensuring that users are content in the space has already been stated. "Corridors do not have to always consist of parallel walls. There are times when it is possible, and desirable, to make corridors dynamic by the modification of one or both sides" (Rengel 225). This could easily be done with an angled wall along one side that would pull people towards opposite ends. Designers could also use angled walls on both sides of a pathway. It would not only create a sense of being "longer than it really is" (Rengel 217), but it could also "help visitors remember whether a particular space is near the narrow or wide end of the corridor" (187). Giving users any assistance in remembering where a space is greatly impacts their ability to navigate the space. Overall, angles are a considerably useful tool in creating gravitational pulls in a building.)

### Curves

Progression could also be affected through the use of curves. Curves are opposite as well as similar to angles. While angles tend to portray sharp movements, "curved lines tend to express gentle movement" (Ching, *Interior Design Illustrated* 95). "Frank Lloyd Wright says the spiral, which mimics the conch shell, allows an infinite line for a circle of movement. He says it's more comfortable for long periods of walking" (Conti 166). Curves can be another great way to encourage movement while adding to visual stimulation. "Associating [curves] with straight or angular forms or placing an element along its circumference can induce in the circle an apparent rotary motion" (Ching, *Architecture* 39). "Curved walls are dynamic and visually active, leading our eyes along their curvature," which in turn would obviously create gravitational pulls (Ching, *Interior Design Illustrated* 33).

### Straights

Straight lines, too, can affect progression. For instance, "straight lines indicate dynamic forward movement opposed to curves" (Harmon 19). This is important because sometimes there is not enough space, a need, or even a want for a curved or angled wall, especially when the design simply needs a swift forward movement. "A space whose length greatly exceeds its width, [such as a hallway], encourages movement along its long dimension" (Ching, *Interior Design Illustrated* 30).

ARCHITECTURAL ELEMENTS:
THRESHOLDS, LAYERS, AND NODES AND SEATING AREAS

Some elements essentially become part of the journey that takes place in a building. Three particular things typically relate to passing through and enhancing progression rather than starting or creating it. This being said these elements are still very important in the process of progression, because even while in motion, people must have reinforcement to keep moving.

### Thresholds

"The threshold is generally regarded as the point of transition from one space to another, that is, the point at which a new experience begins" (Brooker 165). These usually tend to be doorways that connect spaces. "It can indicate the next part of the journey or become a reminder of things already experienced" (164). A threshold, therefore, could move people towards it by showing a glimpse of what is to come should they progress that direction. It could also be an overview of what they are leaving, which could encourage them to move, too, in order to remove themselves from what they were surrounded by. "Thresholds can provide visual links as well as physical" (Brooker 167).

### Layers

Layers are also commonly used in design. This element encompasses hierarchy, both vertical and horizontal, and also addresses the idea of sight lines and their importance in the understanding of interior spaces. Hierarchy plays a very important role in progression in that it emphasizes certain areas, which attracts attention to them. This can be done by raising a plane, depressing it, dropping the ceiling over it, raising the ceiling over it, or simply setting it apart from everything else altogether. Following through with any of these methods will create an area of interest that will attract people.

A point can be made about depressing or raising planes in that it can create sightlines which help to see further through other areas of the building. For instance if a designer chooses to raise a specific area above ground level, even the height of one stair run, it will attract attention to this space which has been given importance. The good thing about its being raised only this high is that one can still easily access it, and it also still allows for sightlines past this raised area to other areas. A raised area is a great alternative to creating a four-walled room that would be hard to orient oneself into and would also block sight lines across the span of the building.

Le Corbusier explained the point of sight lines when he "developed the notion of promenade architecturale, [which is] a carefully orchestrated route that revealed a buildings space's and their overall organization" (Rengel 40). He tended to use this to create an exact path that traveled through the space revealing all its parts, but it could also be understood as simply the importance of being able to at least receive hints of other areas of the building to enhance overall understanding.

### Nodes and Seating Areas

A final yet extremely important element in architecture is that of nodes or seating areas. As previously mentioned it is important for paths to have recurring stimuli so as to not become monotonous, and nodes are a perfect way to address this. "Nodes are important architectural enhancers. They provide relief, encourage social contact, accentuate transitions and entrances, and create memorable spaces along the way" (Rengel 42). In the realm of progression, nodes provide an area of relief that people may gravitate towards, or stumble upon, along their journey as they stop for a while to take a break. "Nodes punctuate the paths of movement through a building and provide opportunities for pause, rest, and reorientation" (Ching, *Architecture* 264). This quote shows again the ability of nodes to provide aid to users in their wayfinding through a space, as well as to offer a moment's relaxation or conversation as needed.

SPACE AS A VOLUME:
CLOSED VS. OPEN SPACES AND SIZE OF SPACES

In addition to paths, one must also consider spatial volumes, which affect how one interacts with a building, including movement through and around the spaces, as well as how they pull people towards or away from a space as a whole.

*Closed vs. Open Spaces*

The first point is that of closed spaces vs. open spaces. Open spaces tend to allow for more gathering, while closed spaces tend to cause people to move away, as though they are not supposed to be there. Even though an open space may attract users, it should also be noted that one must consider the program type and whether an open space is the best option. For instance, "open office plans subject employees to visual, auditory, and olfactory invasions by other workers" (Kopec 14). While this may be quite all right in an interior design office, a room full of accountants trying to grind numbers would probably feel a little different about all the openness for collaboration and discussion. However, once considered, if an open space is still desired there are many ways to achieve this. One way to open up a smaller space is by the addition of windows or doors; they "can help open a space up by providing visual, spatial, and acoustical links to [other] spaces" (Ching, *Interior Design Illustrated* 37). This thinking also refers back to the lighting section in that a designer can draw people towards a space's brightness as well as its vastness. It will also relate later on to the fact that people are attracted to both noise and other people, which will both likely be more present in large open spaces as opposed to tiny closed-off ones.

*Size of Spaces*

Closely related to closed or open spaces is the size of a space. "There is a reaction to being hemmed in as in a tunnel and another to the wideness of the square" (Cullen 170). Sizes of spaces can influence how one feels in the space as well as how one should progress through the space. "The continuity and scale of each path at an intersection can help us distinguish between major routes leading to major spaces and secondary paths leading to lesser spaces" (Ching, *Architecture* 264). This can be helpful to keep people out of private areas, by making those areas smaller. "Distinguishing between main and secondary paths and designing spaces that physically show the difference between the two will produce clear, easier to navigate projects (Rengel 41). People understand this idea because it is much the same as creating their own boundaries where "private property [is] the territory of the individual, and public property, [is] territory of the group" (Hall 10).

Ceiling heights are a big part of the size of a space; a high ceiling compared to a low ceiling makes one feel like he is part of a larger space. Ceiling height can also be used to help with navigation. "Changing the ceiling height within a space, or from one space to the next, helps to define spatial boundaries and to differentiate between adjacent areas" (Ching, *Interior Design Illustrated* 193). This happens because "each ceiling height emphasizes, by contrast, the lowness or height of the other" (Ching, *Interior Design Illustrated* 193).

There also exists a "psychological construct of segmentation bias to cope with long distances" (Kopec 91). Segmentation bias states that "when [one] has to travel greater distances, [he] mentally segments or divides the path into smaller, more manageable sections" (91). Implementation of this idea helps to keep one interested and not overwhelmed. Designers can support segmentation bias by incorporating nodes, material changes, windows, or some element to break up the space so it becomes simpler to understand.

## SPACE PLANNING CONSIDERATIONS: NOISE AND PEOPLE

Space planning is a very important aspect of interior design. It is the part of the design where all creativity and functional knowledge alike are combined to create the rooms and spaces that will make up the building. Consideration must be taken during this design stage to ensure that spaces are placed in a way that is responsive to the needs of the building. It must also be considered what areas match and what areas need to be far away from each other. Navigation comes into play in this because designers must ensure that each space can be accessed and that spaces that need to be near each other are placed that way in the plans. Certain spaces need to be closer to each other based on the amount of noise and people that will usually be associated with that area. Knowing this helps designers avoid creating quiet areas that are constantly disrupted by louder areas.

### Noise

Although noise seems like it would be more of a problem than an assistant in planning interior environments, it can actually be used to help with wayfinding: "The strategic placement of noise-producing zones will assist wayfinding" (Kopec 218). For example, recreation areas usually create a lot of noise, and this noise can attract people to discover what is happening. This thinking is also related to the fact that "what attracts people most ... is other people" (Whyte 348). Many people think this logic is false, and it is, based on what people say, but if one truly watches people, they tend to gravitate towards other people. The "best used plazas are sociable places, with a higher proportion of couples than you find in less-used places, more people in groups, more people meeting people, or exchanging goodbyes" (Whyte 349). This philosophy is mostly related to interaction. People are more likely to go somewhere if there is something or someone there that they can have interaction with.

*****

## CREATING NAVIGABLE SPACES

"It is not enough to see architecture; [one] must experience it" (Rasmussen 33). Designers have an obligation to society to create spaces that are functional as well as pleasing to be in, and in order for a building to be truly functional, one must be able to navigate his way through it. By using the concepts of the different design elements explained previously, one can easily create an environment that causes progression in the wanted directions. Causing progression is very important, and it can also add an exciting challenge to the work of the designer in creating a space using these elements.

Overall, the information of how to use decoration aspects, architectural lines and elements, spatial volumes, and space planning considerations can be used to organize space as well as control how people interact with and progress through the spaces. This is a strong power to have, to be able to control how someone will move, what he will do when he encounters a building. Designers need to understand the seriousness of this control and use it appropriately. "Elaborate wayfinding mechanisms [in design] indicate that a structure or environment is not legible enough on its own" (Kopec 92). Therefore, to create a legible space with good circulation, designers must develop spaces that are understandable and use these control mechanisms to their advantage. Good "circulation causes signage to be a secondary means" (Kopec 91).

Designs should be completed in a way that is organized to the function of a building's needs. If done properly, good circulation will occur, and once the building achieves good circulation, that building becomes a much better, more interesting space that is worthy of experience. "The circulation system has to work both efficiently (particularly in the event of a fire) and aesthetically, offering pleasant surprises, unexpected vistas, intriguing nooks, agreeable lighting variations, and other interesting experiences along the way" (Frederick 73). Designers owe users of building a space that is not only desirable to be in but that works for them and their needs, and this goal definitely includes a space that guides progression through architectural and design elements.

REFERENCES

Birren, Faber. *Color & Human Response*. New York: Van Nostrand Reinhold, 1978. Print.

Bloomer, Kent C., Charles W. Moore, and Robert J. Yudell, *Body, Memory, and Architecture*. New Haven and London: Yale University Press, 1977. Print.

Brooker and Stone. *Form + Structure*. New York, New York: Watson-Guptill Publications, 2007. Print.

Ching, Francis D.K. *Architecture Form, Space, & Order*. Hoboken, New Jersey: John Wiley & Sons, 2007. Print.

---. *Interior Design Illustrated*. Canada: John Wiley & Sons, Inc., 1987. Print.

Conti, Flavio. *The Grand Tour: Individual Creations*. Boston: HBJ Press, 1978. Print.

Cullen, Gordon. "Introduction to The Concise Townscape." *The Urban Design Reader*. Ed. Michael Larice and Elizabeth Macdonald. New York, New York: Routledge, 2007. 167-173. Print.

Frederick, Matthew. *101 Things I Learned in Architecture School.*
Cambridge, Massachusetts: MIT Press, 2007. Print.

Hall, Edward T. *The Hidden Dimension.* New York:
Doubleday & Company, 1969. Print.

Harmon, M.H. *Psycho-Decorating What Homes Reveal About People.*
New York, New York: Simon & Schuster, 1977. Print.

Kopec, Dak. *Environmental Psychology for Design.* New York:
Fairchild Publications, 2006. Print.

Pena, Sierra. Personal Interview. 1 November 2011. Print.

Rasmussen, Steen Eiler. *Experiencing Architecture.* Cambridge:
Massachusetts Institute of Technology, 1962. Print.

Rengel, Roberto J. *Shaping Interior Space.* New York:
Fairchild Publications, 2008. Print.

Whyte, William H. "Introduction," "The Life of Plazas,"
Sitting Space," and "Sun, Wind, Trees, and Water." *The Urban
Design Reader.* Ed. Michael Larice and Elizabeth Macdonald.
New York, New York: Routledge, 2007. 348-363. Print.

Peter D. Fleming is an assistant professor in the Interior Design Department at O'More College of Design. In addition to his sixth year as a professor at O'More, he currently holds the position of Studio Head at McAlpine Booth & Ferrier Interiors in Nashville, Tennessee, and has seventeen years of experience in the architecture and design community. Fleming has been involved in residential interior design all over the country and has vast experience in product design of furniture, lighting, door hardware, and bath fixture collections. Fleming has spent time living and working in New York City and Boston and has had several projects published in such periodicals as *Architectural Digest, Veranda, Southern Accents, The Robb Report, Elle Decor,* and *House and Garden.* Fleming enjoys passing on what he knows to students, as he feels that his education and his former teachers are majorly responsible for where he is now. Fleming holds a Bachelor of Interior Design from Auburn University School of Architecture and has studied at the Institute for Classical Architecture in New York, the Bard Graduate Center of the Decorative Arts, and the Metropolitan Museum of Art.

# THE FUNCTIONALIST IMPERATIVE

## PETER D. FLEMING

*Instructor, Interior Design*
*Head of Design Studio, McAlpine Booth and Ferrier Interiors Nashville*

"Architects, engineers, and Philosophers of the Enlightenment explicitly identified the principles of architecture with those of science, presuming a fundamental analogy in the methods and sources that led all human disciplines to the attainment of truth"
– *Alberto Perez-Gomez*

## SCIENTIFIC OBJECTIVITY

There is no question that creating design solutions with a mindset focused on the principles of division of labor, scientific rationality, and exclusively practical concerns will not generate an efficient process of building or manufacture. The rejection of the poetic and symbolic values of Medieval craftsmanship in favor of those that celebrate the superb functional logic of machinery and manmade form is a design choice like any other that carries significant aesthetic consequence.

An overwhelming focus on geometry and mathematical method that has lost the symbolic dimension in connection to principles of organic order and become principally a descriptive devise and organizing tool can deteriorate into a dogmatic way of thinking. The setting of priorities in building process over aesthetic result (despite abundant resources) offers only the satisfaction of experiencing a room and appreciating it because of the process of conception and execution. This is a level of abstraction rare, and, specific to those more inclined to need order and control, these interiors are easy to recognize. As Louis Sullivan suggests in *Kindergarten chats, 1910*, "He might produce a completely logical result, so-called, and yet an utterly repellent one—a cold, a vacuous negation of living architecture—a veritable pessimism" (32).

In contemporary practice the rational, straight lines of an

International Style influenced design can and do express a self conscious rejection of nostalgic aesthetics and historical styling and can offer an intellectual arrogance as to the refusal to see any worth in what artifacts of previous social conditions and technologies can teach us. We all need to consider where our contemporary notion of modernity will be in fifty years. In the words of Bobby McAlpine, "Modern buildings never look as good as they did when they were first completed, they only decline."

## TECHNOLOGY AND COMFORT

A truly functional design needs to operate efficiently and specifically within its intended purpose. This is a means to an end and is like any good designer serving as the mute enabler of the design for its comfortable and convenient use. A satisfactory solution should not in the end cause any focus at all on the practical, functional task at hand but just work seamlessly and without concern. This is an example of the finer aspects of any design being successful precisely because they are not specifically noticed. We demand from our servants precision and care, decency, and an unassertive presence, regardless of if it is a personal service, the physical extensions of ourselves through the articles we use everyday or machines themselves.

I make this connection through the intense research and development of articles of personal use that have been designed to specifically enhance our bodily comfort and from the anthropomorphic field of physical science which Henry Dreyfuss contributed so much to by documenting and describing the rational application of human physical potentialities in the built environment.

Significant amounts of resources are allocated to bringing to market everything from critical medical equipment to the MAX2 Dual Node Percussion portable massager devised to service our need for low level tactile stimulation. How else can we explain half of the goods on offer at the nearest Brookstone store but to recognize how much effort is put into creating machines to service our needs, however intimate or mundane. Research into bedding is significant, for example, and wholly justified in my view considering the amount of time we actually spend trying to get important rest. The US mattress industry accounted for $5.8 Billion dollars in revenue in 2009 alone.

STYLE
"He is fed on theories: his heart is parched: it is easy for him to wright off an important cycle of emotions, and the multiplicity of arts which give them expression and perpetuate them."
— Le Corbusier (193)

The first task is to consider any notion of modern style as exactly that, a chosen style. One with connotations of technological progress, the dominance of human order over nature, domesticated design, purity, and hygiene when the signature plain white walls are abundant, economic systematization, and, as mentioned earlier, a deliberate and self conscious rejection of historical form. From kitchen appliances to bathroom fixtures to porcelain dinnerware, the sanctity of virginal white rules the contemporary idealism of modernity. Expanses of white walls left empty have the same connotation of luxury as does any rarified object placed in front of it. The space as mute background for the emotive provocations of expressive form in objects, sound, or light.

More purely sculptural investigations through abstract thought as represented in objects or spaces vary a great deal in program and appearance. A relative scale also exists which can be tied to the practical functioning of an object or space from pure abstract object intended for as primarily visual for experiential contemplation to objects of utility styled to reflect a deliberate preference for unadorned surfaces and simplified form.

Early 20th century European modernist style is represented by abstract formal exercises derived from purely sculptural investigations such as the work Kurt Scwitters, the Russian Constructivists, or the Dutch De Stijl. Also through the socio political workers housing of the framers of the Bauhaus ideology, the stripping of material form as an expression of moral purity by Adolf Loos, or the democratized social agenda of the machine made modern form and aestheticized mechanical imagery of material life and a reorganized society idealized in opposition to the established hierarchical tradition of patronage, material, and level of expert craft as epitomized by LeCorbusier. Notions of good design for everyone are politically impossible to disagree with, yet an overly systematized material existence is repressive. The balance is economical and ideological, elitism and novelty are still required conditions for the continued development of design as economy will be expanded upon at first opportunity except for those few willing to forgo the perceived comforts of a physical and emotional life well lived.

Ironically LeCorbusier mentions in *The Decorative Art of Today* when describing the lessons of one of his teachers that nature must be studied beyond its appearance: "Study its causes, forms and vital development" (194). The unifying, underlying principles evident in organic life are lessons ignored at one's peril and prescribe no stylistic response.

## THE SCIENTIFICALLY OBJECTIVE
## IN SERVICE OF ARTISTIC EXPRESSION

"And this power of suggestion, of evoking responsive imagination, is the power of the artist, the poet."
— *Louis Sullivan*

I have to admit that I am partial to the opinion that practical concerns and the technology employed in achieving them are useful primarily in the service of artistic intent. In the conflict between artistic and scientific, interests in design aesthetics are front and center. As interesting and useful as each method of manufacture and the properties of materials are, I find them fascinating only in their artistic potential. The march of technological development will continue opening up ever-unique methods of making, such as three-dimensional printing which will offer even more potential for formal expression just as the computer capabilities have done since the 1960s. This process of technological evolution will never halt, but it should also never be the focus nor operate strictly within any special interest such as the movement towards sustainability, a sincerely moral attempt at affecting the mindset of a generation of designers. Not without merit but not the ethical high ground it is staked out to be either.

Each material, from its raw state to its processing method to its specific working by highly specialized craftspeople, tools, and machinery, offers its own limitations and unique potentialities for expression.

I find it ever gratifying to learn something new about what can be done in any one field because we as designers are, by nature and by necessity, forced to be generalists. We are never without the need to learn more of how to use materials and methods in creating and executing any design; this body of knowledge is vast and offers a lifetime of learning.

Many craft and manufacture techniques are becoming extinct: wood and stone carving; specialty finishes such as eggshell, eglomise, lacquer, specialty painting, and mosaic work are just some of the examples of highly prized, albeit somewhat aesoteric, techniques not being taken up by the next generation of craftspeople or relegated to machine manufacture. The most caustic criticism of the 19th Century was focused on the unbridled use of machinery to replicate the effect of hand workmanship. I mention this not just because I am personally interested in using these methods in contemporary designs but because in their technique themselves there is potent opportunity for inventive re-use in non historical applications. Who is to say the eglomise (the back painting and gilding of glass) has to look anything like a neoclassical design or even be used in traditional applications such as covering case furniture or as decorative wall panels? There really isn't any limit to its style and application except for young designers to recognize its potential in their own contemporary design.

REFERENCES

Le Corbusier. *The Decorative Art of Today.* Cambridge, Massachusetts: MIT Press, 1925. Print.

McAlpine, Bobby. *Personal interview.* June 2010.

McTosh, Jay. "Epperson Expects Faster Industry Growth in 2012, 2013." *Furniture Today* 14 Sept. 2011. Print.

Perez-Gomez, Alberto. *Architecture and the Critics of Modern Science.* Cambridge, Massachusetts: MIT Press, 1983. Print.

Sullivan, Louis. *Kindergarten Chats and Other Writings.* New York: George Wittenborn, 1908. Print.

Shari Fox holds the positions of Vice President of Academic Affairs, Associate Professor of English, and Liberal Arts Department Chair at O'More College of Design; she is also a member of the President's Society of Fellows and Scholars. As a recent participant in the Oxford Summer Research Institute, Fox has a passion for the academic and learning environments. She is particularly interested in educational leadership and has learned the immense value of strong leadership and the willingness to grow and learn.

# A TRULY EDIFYING EDUCATION

SHARI FOX

*Vice President, Academic Affairs*
*Professor and Chair, Liberal Arts*

I HAVE JUST RETURNED from the most amazing experience of my academic life—a research week at University of Oxford. It was a week filled with scholarship, stimulating lectures, conversations with other professors and administrators, and access to one of the world's most renown libraries—the Bodleian—all of this in a legendary and breathtaking city, which is almost exclusively devoted to education.

Whilst there (sorry that you can't hear my new accent!), I visited a number of museums and read some ancient manuscripts. It thrilled me to see how much has been learned and discovered and passed down from this one university. For example, twenty-six British Prime Ministers and over thirty other international leaders, including Indira Gandhi and Bill Clinton, have studied at Oxford. Famous scientists such as Albert Einstein and Stephen Hawking studied and lectured there, and an amazing array of literary figures including J.R.R. Tolkien, C.S. Lewis, T.S. Eliot, Lewis Carol, and many, many more wrote their great works at Oxford. This list goes on to include composers, economists, philosophers, theologians, and medical doctors. Clearly, the University of Oxford has been home to some of the best minds of any time.

Hence, it caused me to marvel at the leisure offered to the many scholars and professors mentioned above. Not leisure in the sense that they had "free time" for entertaining themselves, but a professional leisure to spend their entire careers—paid and housed mind you—pursuing their niche area of interest in academia. I am, of course, delighted that they did, yet it made me realize how this *pure* sort of education differs from so much of the job-seeking education that is pursued today. Indeed, it is very nearly a different approach to education altogether: education for edifying the mind versus education for getting a job.

Note that I said it is *nearly* different, and I must admit that I am of two minds about this apparent conflict. On one hand, I revere and admire the work that many academics have done, and not just on an academic level. Real discoveries that have and do change real lives occur in academic settings. Furthermore, regardless of any practical application, learning and articulating what one has learned nurtures the human spirit. Intellectual growth is fulfilling and beautiful in its own right.

BUT, higher education is becoming extravagantly expensive. One can quite easily spend $120,000 on tuition alone to gain a bachelor's degree in psychology. I do not wish to pick on psych majors as I myself have an undergraduate degree in psychology. It is simply the case that this degree alone does not lead to gainful employment, which is fine IF the student realizes this situation and has other plans for a career or for returning to college for further education. The idea that having a degree automatically equates to a better life is not so automatic.

I attended a lecture at Oxford, given by the President of the University of Puerto Rico, Dr. Rafael Torres. His institution educates over 71,000 students a year, and they are under much scrutiny, as are most institutions of higher education worldwide, to become more accountable to the people, the governments, and the students. He argues that the days when the academy could simply exist on an education for education's sake message is over and that institutions must regain popular and political support.

His lecture ended here and left me wondering how this can be achieved. I believe it is by crafting a new message. Unfortunately, many academics are unwilling to make a new case and are seemingly oblivious to the growing frustrations of tax payers, governments, and students. No doubt our culture has a growing appetite for immediate results, and if higher education does not engage in this conversation quickly, governments and industry will, and they will want quick changes that prove accountability i.e., jobs.

However, higher education is not meant to give students only practical and applicable skills for the work place—that is the role of technical and vocational schools. A bachelor's degree should provide a student with a breadth and depth of knowledge and teach him or her to think more critically, i.e., to analyze data and arguments fully, to think in a coherent and organized fashion, and to articulate thoughts and concepts more easily.

Yet, I will repeat here: higher education is a staggering investment, and most students are not planning to remain in the academic realm but are indeed planning to become contributing members of the work force. They desire a solid and fulfilling career that allows them to live well out in the world. Students need this education to have a solid link to the work place.

This is where I land: pure academia has a place in the world as does pure vocational training, but the largest segment of education should do both. Students need the fulfilling intellectual stimulation of academia as well as some skills and aptitude to find work after college.

It is my vision that O'More College of Design offer just this. Our students should know and understand the basics of the history of philosophical thought as well has how to use industry desirable computer programs. Our students should appreciate and understand the beauty of works of fine art as well as how to use this crucial foundational understanding to craft beautiful and practical designs for the marketplace.

Indeed, this vision must extend beyond mere thought into an articulate message that the O'More community embraces. As demands for accountability grow from both the public and private sectors, we have the opportunity to demonstrate this well-rounded approach to higher education. An approach that develops the mind, that listens to industry need, that responds to government concern, and that, above all, launches our students into successful, fulfilling lives.

Thus, while I will always treasure my time at Oxford, I am quite proud to return to O'More College of Design and work toward honing the vision and this message, and, always the favorite part of my job, working with each and every student to ensure that we are serving them all well and offering them the opportunity of a lifetime.

Kelly R. Gore, IDEC, ASID, is Assistant Professor at O'More College of Design. She is NCIDQ certified in Professional Interior Design and teaches in the Interior Design department where she is able to exhibit her skills in design process and organization. She received a Bachelor of Science in Interior Design from the University of Tennessee School of Architecture and Design.

# America's Dwindling Attention Span and Its Effect on Interior Design

KELLY GORE

*Assistant Professor, Liberal Arts*

A RELATIVE DIAGNOSED with Attention Deficit Disorder at an early age tells a joke, "How many kids with ADD does it take to screw in a light bulb? (I don't know. How many?) Wanna go ride bikes?" Funny, but few would argue against the knowledge that America's population is suffering from a variety of attention-span-related issues. Whether a diagnosed disorder or simply issues of a quickened loss of interest in media topics, several areas of western culture are reflecting the fact that our people require a good deal of manipulation to hold our attention. Wikipedia reports that the average time a person focuses on any one item is eight seconds. (Considering that is near the amount of time it has taken to read the first few sentences of this writing, do I still have your attention?)

Delving a bit deeper, it is important to define "attention span." *Merriam-Webster* defines it as "the length of time during which one (as an individual or a group) is able to concentrate or remain interested."[1] One must additionally consider a few factors: age (neurological development), type of focus (whether visual, auditory, etc.), and the context (informational, graphic, and spatial).[2] There are a variety of resulting time spans, then, that could be considered as average. Nonetheless, those amounts of time are, generally speaking, much shorter than in previous decades. This is apparent in media and life span of "headliners," the turnover of fashion trends, the housing market, and, I believe, in the interior of American homes. While I am not able in this brief writing to explore the causes of this dwindling attention span, I will attempt to delve into its effects on small-scale

---

[1] Merram-Webster.com: "attention span."

[2] Cognitive neuroscience of attention: a developmental perspective, John Edward Richards. Psychological Press, Taylor and Francis e-Library, 2009.

elements as well as large-scale environments.

Most are familiar with the phrase "10 Minutes of Fame." While that specific amount of time might not be accurate, it is indicative of the brevity that any one person or event can capture and maintain our interest. Daniel Gonzalez, a Conversion Rate Optimization (CRO) specialist for a media and marketing website, writes:

> According to most internet marketing experts, you have a total of seven seconds to capture your visitors' attention after they arrive on your web and before they decide to hit the back button and try a different option. Realistically, though, it may be even less, as our age of interactive media and constant advertising messages decrease attention spans even further.

Houman Kargaran, writing for the Epic Design blog, estimates that this number could be much lower:

> Now I don't think 7 seconds rule applies any more. Day by day we are bombarded by advertising which contains images, sounds, videos. In the first 3 seconds if your user doesn't get what she wants she will close the browser window.[3]

Gonzalez goes on to suggest several techniques geared toward capturing our dwindling attention span as it relates to browsing the internet. Attention span, it seems, is such a prevalent issue for site hosts that the marketing realm has CRO specialists, like Gonzalez, who are dedicated to studying the amounts of time users spend on any given site and uncovering those gimmicks that hold our interest for longer than the average 3-7 seconds that is typical!

Industrial design is certainly an example of (if not a reason for) consumer's desire for the next, newer, bigger (or smaller in the case of

---

[3] "5 Types of Killer Website Headlines," Daniel Gonzalez. www.singlegrain.com.

technology), more powerful thing. It took from 1878 until 1949 for the telephone to transition from the wall-mounted box to the free-standing rotary dial phone.[4] (Other sources report that the rotary telephone was introduced earlier, but not made available to consumers until the late 1940s.) In the early 1950s, Western Electric made the rotary telephone available in a variety of colors: lemon yellow, harvest gold, chocolate brown, rose pink, cherry red, lime green, avocado, and others. Prior to this time, the "designer colors" were only available to the most affluent customers.[5] This timeline of seventy-one years is a stark contrast to the design of the cellular telephone. The image below represents a span of little more than twenty years.

It also brings to light the notion of "built-in obsolescence." This term refers to the concept of temporary design—the need to replace one's technology (or other design) more rapidly because it is built to fail. This then breeds an issue with the quality of materials and components. Lack of quality may affect our attachment to objects as well. Ralph Caplan writes of this:

> Paradoxically, our inability to cherish objects is nourished by the technology and economy that provide objects in abundance. One could relate to a wooden table, for one had seen a tree or at least a lumber yard. But how did one relate to a Formica table top? Had anyone seen Formica? Did anyone know what it was? Was it really anything? Did anyone care? The joy we sought (and sometimes even got) in the ding an sich [thing-in-itself] had been supplanted by the satisfaction we build into (and sometimes even get out

---

[4] "The Story of the Telephone" produced by Western Electric.

[5] "A look at the evolution of the dial telephone," Western Electric.

of) the symbol.[6]

A contributing factor to our inability to focus on any one piece of "new" technology for a long period of time could be a result of the manufacturing of fleeting objects. This notion of built-in obsolescence may be the reason for our desire for the next better thing or just another consequence of our ever-shortening interest in any one item for longer than the average cellular telephone contract.

Moving on (perhaps a verbal gimmick to hold the reader's attention), let's look at the turnover of fashion trends over the past several decades. Minor cut and length changes notwithstanding, the outfits worn by women in the decades from the 1920s through the 1940s reveal that most women within the time period wore looks that were quite similar to one another.

Whereas, in the 1960s fashion, pictured below, women's ensembles have notable differentiations in pattern and design (more so than other decades).

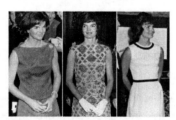

Still, the variety is not extensive when compared with recent years. An interesting note, the "Paper Dress" appears within this decade—a "throwaway" fashion piece that begins to suggest that consumers need not be bothered with quality, timeless apparel. In the 1970s fashion, pictured below, women had a much wider array of clothing choices. Additionally, the variety of materials used to construct the differing garments expanded.

---

[6] By Design, second edition, The Way Things Mean, Ralph Caplan. Fairchild Publications, 2005.

The 1980s and 1990s saw an even greater variety and interest in fashion. One closet might reveal as many as 10 different "personalities" as they related to styles.

The 2000s fashions, pictured below, provided this writer with a difficult task of pinning down all of the styles available to the average consumer. As evidenced by the photographs, there is an unbelievable amount of overlapping trends depicted.

While the earlier decades' pictures lacked variety, they revealed a consistency in style over a wider span of time. The fashions of the future and perhaps even currently will not be revealed in decade spans. The turnover of particular styles tends to happen within a year—each season a "fresh, new" approach to those fashions of the previous season that are so 3-months-ago.

Some might argue that the examples of media, industrial design, and fashion are an unfair categorization of an "issue" given the context. To begin, they are (mostly) affordable commodities and can easily be replaced. (And, if easily replaced, why not move to the next better thing?) Also, the aforementioned designs contextually belong in informational and graphic categories. Therefore, the related information is processed in a part of the brain that operates based on stimuli. It would make sense that, in order to provide appropriate stimuli to trigger this reaction in the brain, we would need variety (or at least that we require it now). What then can be said about the spatial category? What about our built environment? Is it being affected by our dwindling attention span as well? And if so, how do we as interior designers begin to incorporate this piece of the program into an already multi-faceted approach to design?

It would seem that recently Americans have treated their homes as disposable commodities just as their technology or their fashion. While many nostalgic stories are set in one's childhood home, children of the current generation bounce from one home to the next while their parents search for the next best house. Like our industrial designs, the problem could be rooted in quality (or lack thereof) of the available homes. James Kunstler, describing issues related to "the intellectual justification for putting up cheap buildings" notes:

> To aggravate matters, the United States was so affluent after World War Two that we began to regard buildings as throwaway commodities, like cars. They weren't built to last for the ages. So it didn't matter much that flat roofs tend to leak after a few years, because by then the building would be a candidate for demolition. That attitude has now infected all architecture and development. Low standards that wouldn't have been acceptable in our grandparents' day—when this was a less affluent country—are today perfectly normal.[7]

Perhaps our indifference about each house has to do with the indifference in which it was built. As anecdotal evidence of this idea, my husband and I bought our first home in downtown Franklin, Tennessee. We were newly married and freshly graduated from the University of Tennessee's School of Architecture. It was a home built in the 1950s with "good bones" that we slightly modified to make it feel more like ours. Nonetheless, it was a two-bedroom house, and by the time our second child was on the way, we made the decision to transition to a bigger house to accommodate our growing family. The houses available in our price-range were not the well-built homes of the 1950s.

[7] Home From Nowhere, James Howard Kunstler. Touchstone, New York, 1996, p. 145.

They were, instead, quickly-erected suburban homes. We settled on a house, knowing it would not be our "forever home." We sacrificed quality for economy and became transient home-owners, almost immediately dissatisfied with (and detached from) the place in which we dwelt. Our focus was already on to the house we would own after the one we currently owned.

Maybe the resulting interior design is related to this transient state. We now have terminology in our vocabulary such as "builder beige"—the color that one (thankfully, not one designer) chooses that will be the least offensive to most buyers. In our search for that second home I described earlier, we toured one light tan vessel after the next, most of which blurred together in a maddening clump so as not to stand out in any way. I believe at some point we were so bored with the search that we settled on the most convenient rather than the most outstanding. I wonder if the same idea behind "offending the fewest people" leads us to design our homes to appeal to the next potential buyer rather than our own individualized tastes. Certainly the interior architecture is one based on popularity instead of a programmed result of the owner's needs and desires. This is, in fact, the way in which we are taught to design—methodical deciphering of a particular set of criteria to lead to the best possible solution. Instead, homes are not typically designed with a specific client in mind. They are often designed with real estate trends, marketing data, and popularity (read: what everyone else is doing) as the focus, creating yet another something that blends in with everything else. Wow. No wonder we have a dwindling attention span. There is little available that truly captures and holds our attention.

Exacerbating this issue is the availability of "designer" home goods available to consumers at every turn, glamorized and marketed at reasonable prices to a consumer who is inundated with images of what "everyone else" is doing. He or she is coerced into buying stuff under harsh lighting and taking it home to incorporate with that aforementioned tan backdrop. So what if it doesn't work? It hardly matters; it will wear out (or ugly out, as we sometimes say in the industry) in just enough time for the next trend to cross the counters. Who are these "designers" that are creating items for the mass market? They are a whole new generation of people who are engaged in industry-building rather than design itself. Ralph Caplan writes about this issue of design being dealt with in such a broad context:

> They dealt with design in so broad a sense you would have had to be dead not to be interested in the subjects. The [design] papers were a positive critique of civilization. Was this what designers were engaged in?
>
> Unfortunately it wasn't—and still isn't...Before that can happen we need to be saved from "Design," and designers need to be saved from us. By Design I mean what used to be, and too often still is, simplistically called "Good Design"— the expressions of taste manufactured by tastemakers, the collections of certifiably acceptable objects (some of them marvelous indeed) that are the material counterparts of the reading lists approved by the Great Books clubs.[8]

Then, what constitutes the interiors of American homes is, generally, the stuff that is created by economists, these "artificial tastemakers"that have categorized taste as a collective rather than as individual. What is "popular" and mass-marketed dictates an interior that turns over almost as frequently as the shelves at the local big-box store.

What about those interiors that appear more "classic" or "traditional" in nature? Since they're not following the current trend, are they then more closely akin to "Good Design"? I'm not convinced. They are as affected by our lack of attention as their contemporary counterparts. Still a targeted consumer—the shopper who searches for items of that genre—is subject to an equally manufactured symbol of what might have been, but certainly is not now. In his article entitled "Quaintness," Daniel Harris discusses the idea that homeowners of the current generation do not have the "knowledge, patience, or even interest" to create an authentic interior of a particular time period. Rather, they "cobble together a generic past" of items that are mere representations of a myriad of time periods. Much like the restaurants these consumers frequent which offer re-creations of their mélange environments, the home as a result more closely resembles a collection curio with "ten-gallon cowboy hats displayed on the same shelf with

[8] Caplan, p. 10

[9] "Quaintness," Daniel Harris. Design Studies, A Reader, edited by Hazel Clark and David Brody. Berg, 2009. p. 310

colonial milk pitchers, Deco cake mixers with nineteenth-centuryesque [sic] pewter mugs, lava lamps with 'classic wooden replicas of yesteryear's mantel clocks.'"[9] And on the topic of this frequent turnover of interiors, Harris further addresses the manufacturer's role in our depleted interest in any one item for any lengthy time period:

> To ensure that consumers constantly replace their possessions, manufacturers have stigmatized the worn and out-of-date and in the process have produced a world that, out of psychological necessity, purges the environment of objects that betray use, creating a timeless landscape from which all signs of history, of wear and tear, have been eerily eradicated.[10]

And, in a funny twist, Americans tend to pay even more money for interior furnishings and trappings that have been artificially scarred to imitate something that has a history or would be considered time-tested. Fooling almost no one, though, the average consumer of these "artifacts" is constantly driven to replace that item with a more convincing one. This fuels the economy, yes, but it also fuels the cyclical changing of our interior environments.

Is there a resolve to this revolving-door interior that has resulted from our attention deficit issues? Is there a way that designers and consumers alike could remedy faceless, nondescript representations of what could be? I believe, as I have been taught, that accompanying a design degree is a responsibility—yes, the legal responsibility of life, safety, and welfare—but also the responsibility to meet our client's necessities and desires. The programming phase of design is often marginalized and reduced to a listing of space allocations and room assignments. But it is intended to be much more. It is intended to be a careful extraction of personality, character traits, wishes, and dreams. A successful programming would result in an interior environment that nurtures the client—that specific client. The resulting interior would be quite personal rather than general. While some might share similar tastes, few share the same character and history that bring them to that place of differentiation. While we might evolve and require minor shifts and updates on occasion, if our environment is truly a reflection of our

[10] Harris, p. 311

[11] The Architecture of Happiness, Alain de Boton. Vintage International, New York, 2006. p. 263

individuality rather than a generality, it would certainly suggest some longevity. But, this would require a shift in our habitual consumerism…a difficult task, to be sure. Still, as Alain de Botton writes, "Lest we begin to despair at the thought of how much might be required to bring about a genuine evolution in taste, we may remind ourselves how modest were the means by which previous aesthetic revolutions were accomplished,"[11] we have a bit of work ahead. The shift can and should be made to that more enduring interior design that is not a victim of our fleeting attention span.

Dr. Mark Hilliard is the President and CEO at O'More College of Design as well as Professor of Behavior Science. In addition to these titles, he is the Founder of the Hilliard Institute for Educational Wellness, the Founder of O'More Publishing, the Director of the O'More Research Academy, a member of the President's Society of Fellows and Scholars, and the head of the O'More Cultural Field College. He received his Doctor of Arts degree from Middle Tennessee State University and is the published author of three books with his fourth, on Sacred Spaces, currently in progress. Dr. Hilliard spent several trips to Ireland and Cherokee, North Carolina, as well as three fellowships at Oxford University gathering material and research for this article.

# SACRED PLACES AND SACRED SPACES IN DESIGN

DR. K. MARK HILLIARD

*President and CEO*
*Professor, Liberal Arts*

PREFACE

What do the concepts of sacred places and sacred spaces have to do with the field of design, and what can I say, as the author of this article, to convince you to read further and find out? For last year's *Abbey Leix Anthology,* my good friend Dr. John Feehan, Professor of O'More-Ireland and University College Dublin, Ireland, wrote an article entitled "The Spirit of Place: Sacred Character in the Landscape of Laois." County Laois is the homeplace of the O'Mores, and it is a land literally saturated with places believed to be sacred. At least every other year, I lead a group of students on a travel course to Laois, in search of these places.

What, then, is the purpose for a designer to consider such a trip of mind and body, or spirit and soul, into a study of the sacredness of place and space? For an interior designer, the desire should be to understand the relative meaning individuals today and throughout history have given such places. This research of details can then be followed by a consideration of the potential benefits and ability to re-create similar meaning at a new site. For someone studying visual communications, art, fashion design, or other creative fields of design-study, research into sacred places and spaces supports the designer's capacity to better understand the big picture of how design affects our world. Just as all things relate to design, all things also relate to place and space: from words or visuals on a page, to color and design on fabric, or the placement of a window on a building. Through an advancement of knowledge and appreciation for places and spaces that individuals and groups deem as sacred, we better equip ourselves to incorporate appropriate meaning into our designs, be it sacred meaning or simply personal meaning.

This article is the first draft of chapter one, and highlights of additional chapters, of my new book on the topic of sacred places and sacred spaces. This book, like most of my writings, is not meant to be received as irrefutable facts on the subject of sacred places and sacred spaces, but more as an attempt to help myself, and the reader, better understand the mystery of such a topic. In this study don't look for the answer, but rather for possible answers based on factual data, experiential learning, and the ponderings of a mind enchanted by that which is not clear and easily understood.

*Sacred Places and Sacred Spaces* is scheduled to be completed by summer 2012. I will also teach another short-course on this topic in May 2012 and lead another travel group to Ireland in June 2012.

The exploratory research for this study was conducted over fifteen years of travel to the Eastern Band of the Cherokee Reservation, six trips to Ireland, three trips to England, and one trip to France. My studies also included working with a group of O'More College of Design student researchers, through the O'More Research Academy (ORA), and through my teaching a special class on sacred places and spaces over two summers.

Much of the textual research for this study took place at the Bodleian Library at Oxford University, England, while I studied as a summer research fellow and scholar at the Harris Manchester College. Both the historical (and might I say sacred) setting of Oxford and access to the written materials of great minds, provided an enchanting, even mystical, backdrop for learning and writing to occur.

CHAPTER ONE
QUESTIONS OF AUTHENTICITY

In examining a topic like sacred places and sacred spaces I find it fitting to begin with some questions of authenticity and then to examine these questions in the research that follows. I also find it beneficial to attempt to leave behind any pre-conceived notions of what sacred places and sacred spaces are. When we think we know what we are looking for, we often overlook reality in search of myth.

The following are some of the questions that drove and continue to drive my studies:

- do sacred places and sacred spaces exist;
- if they exist, are they reality, or only a part of our imagination and thinking—are they simply a product of emotional and genetic memory, or are they a spiritual phenomenon;
- are sacred places and sacred spaces the same, or do they represent two separate entities;
- do sacred spaces always represent a connection to God or our concept of a higher power, or can they also represent a meaningful connection to the physical and psychological—can places and spaces hold a memory of the past to which we can connect (stored memory);
- if one believes in a universe created by God, is all that is created, in essence, sacred;
- is there a difference in that which is sacred and that which is spiritual;
- can sacred places and sacred spaces be created or recreated by an architect, an artist, or a designer;
- what makes a place or space sacred;
- are there common physical elements located at sacred sites;
- what is it we connect with at a sacred place or space—a power, an entity, an emotion, a past-presence, God;
- what helps us connect or hinders us from connecting;
- why do some people connect and others do not; and
- does the sacred reside within the place, the space, or the one encountering the place or space?

To begin to understand the theory of sacred places and sacred spaces and these related questions, it is important to first understand the various meanings behind the three terms: sacred, places, and spaces. It is likewise important to value the fact that individuals approach this subject from a variety of stances. Some approach it from a religious standpoint with God as the divine source of all that is sacred, others from a metaphysical or spiritual standpoint that may or may not involve religion and one's sense of God, and some from more of a physiological or psychological (physio-psycho) point of view with the concept of what we perceive as sacred to be understood within the realm of science and the physical makeup of our world. I will attempt to address each of these views in the chapters that follow.

# CHAPTER TWO
## SACRED OR SPIRITUAL

### The Sacred

The Sacred, by definition, is that which is special, unique, personal, honorable, consecrated, or holy. It implies a positive purpose and is something you don't try to change or conform to the norm. It is sanctified or set apart and, therefore, to be respected—even if not understood. In fact, that which is sacred is not meant to be understood as we understand customary knowledge and practices, but it is to be studied and revered with a higher knowledge that is anything but standard.

### The Spiritual

That which is spiritual is "of the spirit." In practical terms, it means spirit-ritual—ritual or activity that involves the spirit. This spirit can be the spirit of humankind or the spirit or spiritual essence of nature and the creation. It can also involve spiritual entities and energies that are not of nature or humankind—supernatural entities that never had physical life—and spiritual entities that once had physical life but have that life no longer—past living entities that have died. While the term spiritual typically carries a positive definition, it can also be used as a negative term involving spiritual evil and death.

### Sacred Vs. Spiritual

Is everything that is spiritual, sacred? And is all that is sacred, spiritual? My response to this question did not come until toward the end of the study. My findings: a spiritual thread runs through all that is sacred. The sacred, therefore, must have a spiritual component in order to be sacred. This spiritual component for the sacred might first be observed as a physical or psychological stimulation (chapter four), but it has the action of a spiritual energy source behind it. The spiritual, on the other hand, may or may not be sacred. Sacred implies a positive force, a higher purpose. Something on the level of the spiritual may or may not have this positive force or higher purpose. The spiritual thread that runs through life can transport both evil and positive spiritual energy. Spiritual energy that is evil, or negative, is not sacred. The use of the spirit for non-worthy purposes is not sacred. Sacred places and spaces, therefore, are not the same as haunted places and spaces (based on the definition of haunted as negative spiritual energy). This does not preclude the possibility that sacred sites can present spiritual entities, it simply implies that at a sacred site, these entities are positive.

CHAPTER THREE
SACRED AS A RELIGIOUS OR DIVINE TERM

From a religious or divine perspective, that which is sacred involves the heavenly, the holy, and the Godly, rather than the physical, the mundane, the genetic, or the earthly. "Sacred space is to celebrate God first, and only then to provide nourishment for the worshiper" (North, 2007, p.31). On a practical level this entails any of these three elements: that which is *of God*; that which is *from God;* or that which is *set apart for God.*

Of God—the fruit of God's Spirit (joy, peace, love, forgiveness, patience, kindness, goodness, faithfulness, etc.)—qualities of God bestowed upon man, or other elements of creation, as an outgrowth *of God* or God's Spirit residing within (Holy Bible, Galatians, Ephesians). These characteristics are not a common product of man's genetic, survivalistic, natural instinct but are acquired as man and creation become reacquainted and reconnected with their creator.

From God—gifts from God (the created world, life, breath, food, family, friends), meaning the created world and the things God gives the created word to sustain it and show His love for it.

Set apart for God—anything we wish to dedicate to God, or that He has dedicated (our lives, our money, our family, an activity, a day, a place, or a space).

At this level of the sacred, it may perhaps be said that all that is created by God is sacred because it is made up of "God Stuff." He spoke, He breathed, He said, He asked, He commanded...and it was so. God as a creator is not to be viewed as a magician, creating illusions from nothing, anymore than an artist's painting or sculpture is magic, but rather God created and creates everything from Himself, from His actual energy and existence. God's creation is His poem, His song, His story, His painting. God is the original artist of all that is natural. Thomas Acquinas expressed this conviction of all things beginning from an original source as "First Cause." All things have a cause—something that put it into motion, into play, except First Cause, which started it all. Within this pattern of thought it can well be conceived that all that was/is created has spirit or spiritual essence because it all began with and from God, who is Spirit.

I must interject that my use of the term *religion* alongside the word *divine* for this category is more a matter of individual perception as a commonly accepted "God term." I, however, believe the word religion has been misconceived to portray an institutionalized form of spiritual/ social activity that has too often conformed to nothing more than a physical/social methodology. The term religion as seen in its most common form today is not, in-fact, the best way to interpret a divine God. However, the original meaning for the term religion as noted by Biblical text is "pure and undefiled religion in the sight of our God and Father is this: to visit orphans and widows in their distress, and to keep oneself unstained by the world" (James 1:27). This description denotes God as working through man to accomplish His divine and sacred purposes—meeting of the needs of others and not allowing the physical world to control us. He interjects humankind with abilities that we cannot obtain on our own merit.

A larger umbrella (than the term religion) under which all that is sacred corresponds are the words metaphysical and spiritual. If humankind has a spirit and a soul (and I use the word spiritual to include both), then we can exhibit these entities through a variety of means: in our religion; our art; our attempt to find meaning and purpose in live; our sharing ourselves (our gifts and talents) with others; and our experiencing nature and all that is created.

CHAPTER FOUR
SACRED AS A METAPHYSICAL OR SPIRITUAL TERM

That which is metaphysically or spiritually sacred is on the level of the mystical, the unexplainable, the extraordinary, rather than the natural, the logical, or the ordinary. It cannot be described or understood with commonplace words or activities, nor can it be appreciated with the routine mental processes of the mind apart from the spirit. "Sacred places and spaces are full of history and people's emotional attachments to or memories of them. Perhaps sacredness lies not in the actual places, buildings, or locations, but in the hearts and spirits of the people who visit these sites" (Corley, Martha, Sacred Places—Sacred Spaces Class, 2010). In his journal on July 16th 1851, Henry David Thoreau (1993) wrote, "What temple what fane what sacred place can there be but the innermost part of my own being" (1851).

This is not to say that the sacred lies only within the individual (within the spirit and soul of man), but at the level of the metaphysical, the sacred is a combination of the sacredness of the inner spirit and soul of humankind and a connectivity of this essence with the spiritual or sacred component of all that was/is created by God. And conceivably this sacredicity can extend to that which is also created by man—does humankind have the ability to insert individual spiritual essence into something we make or into that with which we have intimate contact?

That which is sacred on this level often involves something that is set apart for a higher purpose that may, on the surface, have a physical objective, but this physical objective has spiritual significance. This level of the sacred may or may not specifically relate to one's concept or understanding of God or the divine, but it does relate to the concept of spirit or inner essence—a personal drive to seek out meaning and purpose through metaphysical or spiritual thought and action. The higher purpose could be to make the world a better place through spiritual activity like caring for the needs of our family and others we love. It could involve the use of spiritual elements to connect spiritually—praying, singing, meditating, finding a personal spiritual or sacred place, or using various holy implements (these methodologies may also be used for divine sacred activity). Or it may take place by visiting and connecting with recognized sacred sites in order to uncover their mystery. The seeker, however, may not be aware of the spiritual motivation behind such action.

The metaphysically sacred is full of mystery. If we overlook the mystery and only see the obvious (the observable facts, or what we perceive to be apparent), we can miss much of what is there to greet us, to charm us, to enchant us. This level of the sacred allows us to, at least for a moment, be transported beyond the physical limits of time and space.

Though most have experienced this phenomenon at some time, our question often remains: was the spirit, the soul, the mind, or the body actually transported beyond the level of the physical, or was it, is it, more a state of emotional transcendence? If that which is sacred merely transports our mind and body from its ordinary thoughts and actions to higher levels of thinking and responses, but still within the confines of our self-limiting physical mind and body, this level of the sacred is merely physiological or psychological. But, if our spirit and soul can reside within our mind and body and at the same time be transported to a higher, non-physical plane, it is a metaphysical phenomenon.

CHAPTER FIVE
SACRED AS A PHYSIOLOGICAL OR PSYCHOLOGICAL TERM

That which is sacred on the level of the physical or psychological has the ability to draw us in, to entice us, to touch us through elements of a physical nature. This physical or psychological impression of the sacred is one that creates emotions, a sense of awe, and high levels of multi-sensory stimulation. The stimulation often begins at the level of the mind or the body, but by those approaching it from a religious, divine, metaphysical, or spiritual standpoint, it is believed that this physical stimulation is meant to move us toward a higher level of thinking (to that which is spiritual or sacred): such as the use of stained glass windows, sacred music, poetry, art, light, a building, or a meaningful historic site to stimulate the physical, then the spiritual. Within this viewpoint, these physical and psychological elements can put us in the mood, so to speak, for spiritual or sacred activity to take place. The Cherokee referred to this staging process as pre-ceremonial ritual or pre-ceremonial preparation that may or may not be entered into consciously. Sometimes we set the stage for metaphysical activity to occur. At other times it simply happens to us, unexpectedly.

Think of this example. You are stressed out from a busy week. It is Sunday morning, and you are trying to get the children ready for church service. You are running late and finally arrive at the church building already exhausted and in a bad mood. Are you physically and mentally prepared to worship? No. Are there physical elements of the site, the building, or the landscape that can help prepare you to switch gears from your physical thinking to spiritual thinking? There should be. Is there splendor in the simplicity of design (an old historic church with wooden pews, a mountainside auditorium of nothing more than stones, trees, and earth upon which to sit) or magnificence in the architectural beauty of design (a grand cathedral, stained glass windows exploding with sunlight, color choices that set a psychological and even a spiritual mood) that assists with this physical to metaphysical transition? The fact is, we need there to be such design. The specific place nor the design is required, and it is not to be worshiped, or overly valued, but it does provide a great advantage in preparing our spirit, soul, mind, and body for something sacred to occur.

One of the most common understandings of this physio-psycho level of the sacred is the theory that various elements of physical existence have the ability to store memory—a piece of furniture, a building, a grave site, or a place in history where something significant has taken place, etc. As we encounter the element(s), we also have the opportunity to encounter the memory, something we as individuals may or may not have the psychological ability to achieve or understand.

This memory may simply be a product of cognitive recall: "When something is sacred it holds special meaning for you, like a garden that you have worked on all spring in order to relax and maintain, a song that you cannot let go of because it makes you happy, or even looking at a special place that holds value, not in the sense of money, but the value of love and respect" (Joy, Travis, Sacred Places—Sacred Spaces Student, 2010). Or it may have a much deeper connection to our metaphysical existence: "What is it about a place that awakens the sense that divinity breathes in this place more than elsewhere? Why is there a stillness in some places that allows the questions that set us aside from other animals to rise to the surface of our busy minds? Perhaps in them, we find a 'collective unconscious echo of memory'" (Feehan, John, p. 78).

Whether the result of natural design, purposeful man-made design, mystical design, or design through stored memory and the history of place, humankind benefits in the search for the sacred by coming in physical contact with sacred places and sacred spaces. The more we experience such sites, and the more we begin to research and understand their background, their original meaning, and their individual meaning for self, the more opportunities we have to discover and experience the sacred.

Chapters Six through Fifteen will include
The Sacred and History
The Sacred and the Senses
The Sacred and Ritual
Qualities of Sacred Encounters
What is Place
What is Space
Sacred Places
Sacred Spaces
Sacred Sites: Sacred Places and Sacred Spaces as One
And a Sacred Places—Sacred Spaces Companion Journal

REFERENCES

Corley, Martha. (2010). Sacred Places—Sacred Spaces Class, Student Paper.

Feehan, John. (2010). "The Spirit of Place." *Abbey Leix Anthology. Vol 1.* Franklin, TN: O'More Publishing, p. 78.

Holy Bible, New American Standard Version. (1995). Grand Rapids, Michigan: Zondervan Publishing House.

Joy, Travis, (2010). Sacred Places—Sacred Spaces Class, Student Paper.

North, Philip & North, John. (2007). *Sacred Space: House of God, Gate of Heaven.* London: Continuum Books, p. 31.

Thoreau, Henry David. (1993). *Henry David Thoreau, A Year in Thoreau's Journal: 1851.* London: Penguin Books.

Rachel Kirk in an instructor of fine arts at O'More College of Design as well as a part-time Art Foundations faculty member at the Art Institute of Tennessee-Nashville. She attended the University of Tennessee, Knoxville, where she received a Master of Fine Arts in Painting and Drawing. Kirk's work has been exhibited regionally and nationally and has been included in numerous private and public art collections.

# A CIRCLE OF ART

RACHEL HALL KIRK
*Instructor, Fine Arts*

MOST PEOPLE ARE LUCKY if they find one calling in life. I've found two: art and teaching. I've been lucky enough to combine the two for over eight years and learn firsthand how strongly each can reinforce the other.

## I DRAW, THEREFORE I AM

I've been an artist since I can remember. One of my earliest and fondest memories is from 1st grade, when I was out of school for the day and I went to work with my dad, who taught high school. While he taught I sat in his office, and drawing kept me occupied. Throughout that day several of my father's students came in to check on me, and they were all greatly impressed with my drawing ability. Their interest in my drawings gave me confidence and a sense of gratification that I had never felt, and that, in turn, inspired my lifelong development into an effective artist and educator.

A keen eye for shapes and value has helped immensely in my development as an artist, but being an excellent copier only goes so far. A student of art has to be taught to draw adequately enough to convey ideas, for ideas are where the artistic process bears fruit. Although I consider myself to be a consummate draftswoman, I don't assume that technical skill alone will produce quality work.

Even though my work is abstract, my background as a realist influences my current work in the form of tenacious mark-making and attention to detail. The physical act of drawing repetitious shapes, marks, and colors is the closest activity I've found to meditation, and as a result my art-making process is soul-nourishing. In the last few years I've been focused on a body of work based on patterns found in nature. Insects have been the greatest source of inspiration. I have collected and studied the bodies of bees, wasps, and spiders, and use the designs and colors on their bodies as a launching point for my abstract designs. The shapes and forms of their webs, hives, and nests are also inspiration, as are the patterns found within their tissues—I often study the insects under a microscope.

Sometimes I think of my studio practice as if it were a science laboratory. I keep specimens in jars so I can later study them under a microscope. I enjoy methodical evaluation of the objects I draw; as a scientist would study a dissection, my drawing process requires study of the subjects in close proximity. The process of mixing paints and other materials contributes to that laboratory environment as well, because I often mix materials that do not go together, such as oil-based and water-based products, in order to see what the results will bring. These materials experiments can sometimes yield interesting and unexpected results with texture and color.

I (ALSO) TEACH, THEREFORE I AM

Though I fell in love with art first, a passion for education is just as integral to my makeup. I strive to teach with the same energy, passion, creativity, respect, patience, care, and thoughtfulness as the inspirational educators from whom I was lucky to have learned. My father, brother, grandmother, and aunt have collectively spent over a century as public school teachers. (Even my stepmother is a teacher.) My enthusiasm for teaching comes naturally. Teaching is in our blood.

I have held a variety of positions at several colleges and universities here in Tennessee since receiving my Master of Fine Arts degree eight years ago. What drew me to college teaching, and what keeps me coming back, is a combination of the maturity, the academic rigor, and the variety of the students in a given classroom.

Many of my college students work their way through school. Some of them are a little older than the traditional straight-from-high-school teenager and have already had successful careers in another field. Some tackle the responsibility of raising children while going to school. Every classroom of students is different, but one constant is maturity.

One part of my job that keeps me on my toes is the fact that no two days are exactly alike. Students are naturally curious, so they often ask challenging questions and pose complex ideas that keep me engaged and excited. I truly believe that successful teachers constantly learn as they teach, especially in a rigorous academic environment.

My youngest student ever was 17 years old, and my oldest student was in his mid-eighties, with a wide range of ages in-between. That elderly student was the perfect example of the richness of the college environment. I learned as much from him as he did from me, and his fellow students benefited greatly from listening to his life stories and witnessing his lifelong commitment to personal betterment through continuing education.

As a foundation level art instructor, I teach a lot of first-semester freshmen. Many of these students have never lived away from home or enjoyed any degree of independence. The freedom that the college experience allows can often be overwhelming, and without the proper support and guidance new students can get lost and give up. I understand this and aim to give my students enough guidance to keep them on track while also respecting their independence by giving them room to explore and grow.

As an educator and mentor in the microcosmic safety bubble of a college setting, I'm one of the final few on a long list of people who have influence over the students before they enter the "real world" outside of academia. I wholeheartedly accept my role, and I do everything I can to help prepare my students for their respective careers.

At the end of my course, serious and successful students will leave with good craftsmanship skills. They will be able to speak logically, clearly, and critically about their work and the work of others. They are efficient and have time-management skills. They are aware of the current industry trends. And they understand how to develop ideas from conception to completion.

I always make a point to show my own artwork to my students. My intention is to show them that I am a working artist who is engaged in professional work outside of the academic environment. I want to lead by example, and if they see that I pursue gallery exhibitions, it might encourage them to be proactive in their careers.

AND THE TWO GO HAND IN HAND

I have seen firsthand the impact that an effective teacher can have on a student. I once had a student tell me that all students have a spark of a flame inside them, a spark that is often extinguished by uncaring professors. She then told me that I feed that spark and turn it into a fire.

My students often serve the same purpose for me whether they realize it or not. They inspire me all the time to work harder in my studio practice. Seeing them use unexpected color combinations, or a stunning mixture of materials, reminds me that I need to experiment and evolve artistically. Perhaps most importantly, their enthusiasm is infectious. It can be easy to fall into a rut of making the same painting year after year, and seeing my students work creatively helps me to avoid that pitfall in my own artistic life.

Conversely, my studio practice has a direct and positive impact on my teaching effectiveness. Just like a chef needs to keep his knives sharp, I need to maintain my technical skills. When I work on my own art it helps to sharpen those skills so I can walk into the classroom at any time with confidence and ability. From the studio to the classroom back to the studio again—it's one big circle of art.

Jessica Langdon graduated in 2009 from Lipscomb University with a degree in business management before pursuing her degree in interior design at O'More College of Design. She has served an internship at The W Group as part of her design studies. This writing is part of her final paper in Research and Documentation, a senior level course at O'More, and was nominated for publication in this anthology by her department chair.

# CENTRIPETAL AND CENTRIFUGAL SPACES:
## HOW COLOR, LIGHT, AND SPATIAL ORIENTATION DEFINE HUMAN INTERACTION

JESSICA LANGDON
*Student, Interior Design*

INTRODUCTION

"Architecture is so essentially a social art that no architect can talk about his medium or about his schemes without reference to how they will be used by people; and a good deal of the conscious intention behind any design, as well as various decisions about its elements, are expressed in terms of its consequences for social behavior" (Gutman 340). The goal of architecture and design is to create functional, usable spaces that suit users' needs. How each person interacts with a space is highly subjective and varies among individuals. While reactions to a space may vary, individuals basically follow the same series of steps to first analyze a space and then react to it. By understanding how individuals process and react to a space, designers can create spaces that encourage or discourage interaction. Spaces that encourage or discourage interaction will be referred to as centrifugal and centripetal, respectively.

Centrifugal and centripetal were adjectives used to describe a study of light conducted by Faber Birren, a renowned color expert. He explained centrifugal light as increasing activity, alertness, and outward orientation. Conversely, he described centripetal light as focusing one's attention inward (31). Birren's use of vocabulary does not relate to physical movement within a space but rather to how an individual interacts psychologically and physiologically within a space. Although the terms centrifugal and centripetal are typically related to the study of physics, this research will refer to centrifugal and centripetal in more abstract terms. Centrifugal spaces, in this research, will refer to spaces that encourage interaction with the environment and others in the environment. Centripetal spaces will refer to spaces that encourage reflection and inward focus. Multiple design elements can encourage centrifugal and centripetal spaces including color, light, and spatial orientation.

## INTERACTION WITH SPACE

Before beginning to shape a space, one has to understand how spaces are experienced. Four situational factors—occasion, players, resources, and surroundings—can describe the context of activity for a space and provide implications for design to enrich an experience (Rengel 28). An occasion refers to a specific event taking place that requires an expected set of behaviors. The players are anyone involved in the occasion. In a restaurant, this could include patrons, wait staff, managers, and chefs. In a school, the players could include everyone from teachers and students to parents and cafeteria workers. The resources could be physical, like space and equipment, or intangible, like time and money (28).

Surroundings define the space itself, but users can distinguish between surroundings directly related to the occasion and those that are peripheral in close proximity (Rengel 31). Two of these factors, occasion and players, are usually perceived similarly by users of the space, while the other two factors, resources and surroundings, may be perceived differently by individual users. Regardless, the combination of factors will be perceived uniquely by each individual, complicating the intended perception of a design (31). "It is important to stress the fact that the individual's behavior is guided not only by the goals he seeks, but also by his cognitive processes, that is, by the way he reads and interprets or even imagines his environment" (Proshansky 174). Interior design aims to alter surroundings and resources to suit the needs of the players in an occasion. Surroundings and resources that have the most impact in design include color, light, and spatial orientation.

While an individual's reaction to a space is subjective, "the basic chain of events consists of a given environment experienced by a person, the person's processing of the conditions presented by the place and situation, and the person's behavioral reaction, be it jumping with excitement or running in disgust." (Rengel 29). Albert Mehrabian and James Russell created a framework for deriving how an individual will react to a particular environment. They equated the emotional reaction to a space with three measurements: arousal, pleasure, and dominance. Arousal refers to the amount of stimulation one perceives. High levels of arousal can lead to increased blood pressure and energy. Low levels of arousal can make one feel fatigued or lethargic. Pleasure simply refers to the amount of enjoyment one derives from the space. A high level of pleasure could be observed through happiness, smiling, and a jovial attitude. A low level of pleasure would be indicated by withdrawal and sadness. Dominance indicates how much control or influence one has over a space (29). They concluded that the combination of only the three elements could lead to a variety of reactions. "Depending on [one's] reaction, [he] will be more or less likely to approach, or avoid, the environment" (29).

COLOR

The first component to be applied to centrifugal and centripetal design is color. Color, considered by artists and designers as one of the most influential elements of design, has been explained by psychologist Ulrich Beer as creating a certain and unavoidable psychological reaction: "Seldom, surely, is the psychological part of an appearance in nature so great as it is in the case of color. No one can encounter it and stay neutral. We are immediately, instinctively, and emotionally moved. We have sympathy or antipathy, pleasure or disapproval within us as soon as we perceive color" (11). While many reactions to color are subjective and depend on one's personal experiences and associations, a number of scientific studies have proven that characteristics of color relate similarly to all individuals.

In 1994, Patricia Valdez and Albert Mehrabian conducted a series of studies analyzing the effects of hue (the color itself), saturation (intensity), and brightness (value) (394). Their studies concluded that pleasure was determined by brightness and saturation, with more influence directed by brightness. A second aspect of their research analyzed the effects of specific colors using Munsell color chips, which define colors using hue, value, and chroma (color purity) (Cleland). "Blue, blue-green, green, purple-blue, red-purple, and purple were the most pleasant; whereas yellow, green-yellow, and red-yellow were the least pleasant; with red being rated at an intermediate value of pleasantness" (Valadez and Mehrabian 406).  Green-yellow and yellow also led to feelings of dominance, whereas red-purple led to feelings of submission (406).   Furthermore, Valdez and Mehrabian generalized that "dark colors are more likely to elicit feelings that are similar to anger, hostility, or aggression" (408).  Their overall conclusion was that the effect of color depended more on the saturation or brightness of a color than the hue itself.  These findings were reiterated by Kenneth and Cherie Fehrman in *Color: The Secret Influence*: "With regard to excitement or arousal, the intensity of the color appears to be of greater significance than the color itself" (81).

PSYCHOLOGICAL AND PHYSIOLOGICAL EFFECTS OF COLOR
    Although the preceding studies place little importance of the actual hue, multiple studies have recorded psychological and physiological effects of specific hues.  "Environmental color has a powerful impact on the human body and mind, but most of the time they are experienced with an astonishing lack of awareness" (Holtzschue 4).  Faber Birren describes some of the reactions to color: "Color affects muscular tension, cortical activation (brain waves), heart rate, respiration, and other functions of the autonomic nervous system— and certainly that it arouses definite emotional and esthetic reactions, likes and dislikes, pleasant and unpleasant associations" (20).
    Red has long been known to be a symbol of love and life (blood), but it is also known for its "qualities of high energy and passion" (Marberry and Zagon 16).  Red's inherent energy explains why it has been described as arousing, exciting, and stimulating, linking it to elevated blood pressure, passion, aggression, rage, and intensity (Marberry and Zagon 16, Mahnke 61).  Orange, a bright, stimulating, cheerful color, is known for its "qualities of emotion, expression, and warmth" (Marberry and Zagon 16).  In low to moderate saturation levels, orange is interpreted as jovial, lively, energetic, extroverted and sociable.  In high saturation levels, orange can become intrusive and blustering (Mahnke 62).  Brown, a member of the orange family, personifies comfort and security.  Its earthly quality symbolizes stability and dependability.  The wrong shade of brown, however, can be "glum, grubby, and drab" (Mahnke 62).  Yellow, inherently cheerful and

optimistic, symbolizes clarity and intellect. Its cheery nature invokes imagery of hope, wisdom, and a bright future (Mahnke 62). In certain nuances, yellow's mood-enhancing ability could adversely connote aging (Marberry and Zagon 16). High levels of saturation can also present yellow too strongly, leaving an impression of egocentricity (Mahnke 62).

Green's complimentary relationship to red on the color wheel automatically requires it to be symbolic of healing (Marberry and Zagon 16). Because the colors are opposite one another on the color wheel, the perceived effects from each color should also be opposite. Green is often seen as a color of relaxation, tranquility, refreshment, quiet, and nature. An incorrect shade of green, however, can come across as envious, common, tiresome, or guilty (Mahnke 63). Blue is also known for its qualities of relaxation and serenity. It invokes feelings of calmness, security, loyalty, comfort, sobriety, and contemplation. Blue can also be linked to passivity, quietness, cleanliness, mental reflection, sea, and sky. Conversely, blue is related to melancholy, depression, sadness, and yearning (Marberry and Zagon 16, Mahnke 63-64). Shades of purple and violet are generally linked to meditation and spirituality, automatically classifying these colors as creating feelings of inner calm and stress reduction (Marberry and Zagon 16). Historically linked to royalty, purple can be seen as regal, dignified, exclusive, strong, sensual, and intimate. Negatively, purple can be lonely, mournful, pompous, unsettling, narcotic, or morbid (Mahnke 64). White, a symbol of purity, holiness, and spirituality, also represents goodness, peace, cleanliness, and light. In both positive and negative connotations, white is seen as sterile (64-65). Black is most commonly associated with darkness, grief, death, and fear, but it is also related to power, status, elegance, dignity, and richness (65-66). Gray, a conservative, quiet, and calm color, can be dreary, tedious, passive, and lacking energy (66).

Studies have concluded colored light has similar measurable effects as pigments. In *Gesertz der Farbe* (Laws of Color), Heinrich Frieling presents an investigation of colored light that includes both physiological and psychological reactions. He found red light to be arousing but leading to inconstant blood pressure, increased pulse, headaches, and an unpleasant feeling of tightening of the throat.

Yellow light is described by research subjects as "mighty" and "sunlike" but does not necessarily lead to feelings of pleasantry or calmness (Mahnke 39). Violet-blue light, however, is found to be pleasant, restful, and good for concentration. Lastly, green light is found to be pleasant, agreeable, and more calming that red. Subjects, though, found it to be compelling (Mahnke 39).

While generalizations can be made about the effects of color, the experience of color is highly subjective. How one experiences color depends on personal associations and experiences. Scientists specializing in clinical psychology have concluded that color is the most significant factor leading to emotional response. Maria Rickers-Ovsiankina, a scientist who worked with the Rorschach ink-blot method, writes about such:

> Color experience, when it occurs, is thus a much more immediate and direct sense datum than the experience of form. Form perception is usually accompanied by a detached, objective attitude in the subject. Whereas the experience of color, being more immediate, is likely to contain personal, affectively toned notes. (Birren 29)

David Katz, a German-Swedish psychologist who worked primarily with the perceptions of environment, explains, "Color, rather than shape, is more closely related to emotion" (Birren 29). Frank Mahnke, founder and director of the American Information Center for Color and Environment, echoes the same observation in *Color, Environment, & Human Response:* "A color impression is not only a mechanism of seeing, but also a sensation or feeling that simultaneously activates our thoughts and our cognitive mechanism" (7).

EFFECTS OF LIGHT

Light is the second component of defining a centrifugal or centripetal space. "Visual acuity for color, hormonal responses to color, adaptation, and synaesthesia are physiological and involuntary responses of the body to a stimulus of light" (Holtzschue 39). Directly related to how an individual perceives an environment, light can fulfill Mehrabian's determined environmental need for stimulation. Stimulation, previously described as arousal, is a psychological need that can be fulfilled by appropriate lighting (Winchip 327). An appropriate amount of stimuli "can increase attentiveness, reduce fatigue, alter perceptions of time, and promote positive moods" (327). Positive light stimulation can be achieved through using "varying light levels, using nonuniform lighting patterns, and having windows with views" (327). The opposite is true with too much stimulation. Overstimulation, "derived from glare, flickering, unnatural light patterns, noise, or color distortions," can cause sensations of discomfort, irritability, dissatisfaction, and lack of safety (328). Absence of light can have similar effects to overstimulation. Dark spaces cause users to feel nervous, anxious, and generally uneasy, especially in an unfamiliar place or during an emergency. Designers can alleviate these pressures through adequate use of wayfinding lighting and signage (328).

NATURAL LIGHT

Natural light has been proven through scientific studies to have an impact on individuals. In addition to providing a "view and ventilation, daylight also has positive psychological and physiological effects on individuals by reducing stress...and encouraging positive attitudes" (Winchip 27). Photobiological researcher Dr. Richard J. Wurtman stated in Scientific American, "Visible light is apparently able to penetrate all mammalian tissues to a considerable depth" (qtd. in Fehrman and Fehrman 67). Wurtman's statement suggests "that each of the various effects of light on mammalian tissues has either a direct or an indirect effect; but it has an effect, even though we may not be aware of it" (Fehrman and Fehrman 67). Natural light's effect on mammals in more reliant on color temperature than its source. The same effect can be achieved through artificial lighting. In contrast to typical harsh fluorescent lighting, warmer, softer lamps mimicking natural light should be used to stimulate the same biological reactions.

LIGHTING PREFERENCES

A study of light preference by Flynn (1977) "indicate[s] that people prefer warm and dim lights, compared to cool and bright sources" (Winchip 326-27). Birren explains this preference through "centrifugal action" (31). He describes centrifugal action as color and light focusing an individual's attention outwards, or more simply, causing one to be more extroverted and interactive. This phenomenon occurs with "high levels of illumination of warm and luminous colors (such as) yellow, peach, and pink" (31). Centrifugal action creates "increased activation in general, alertness, (and) outward orientation. Such an environment is conducive to muscular action, effort, and cheerful spirit" (31). With lower levels of illumination, softer surroundings, and cooler hues, Birren determines that centripetal action results. Centripetal action focuses one's attention inward. Cooler hues of gray, blue, green, and turquoise create less distraction and encourage better concentration on "difficult visual and mental tasks" (31).

Birren's observations are confirmed by a nineteenth century study conducted by Americans S. Pancoast and Edwin Babbit. The Pancoast/Babbit study observes the effects of red light versus blue light on the nervous system. Their findings conclude that the red light consistently "accelerated the Nervous System" while the blue light consistenly "relaxed the Nervous System" (Mahnke 6). Kenz (1995) conducted a study analyzing "the effects of various electrical light sources on mood and cognition of males and females" (Winchip 326). Warm light (3000K) decreased negative moods and problem-solving skills of women, and both these things were increased in cool light (4000K). The opposite was true for male subjects. However, "warm light generated positive moods for both genders" (326-327).

SPATIAL ORIENTATION

The third component that can shape a centrifugal or centripetal experience is spatial orientation, defined as how design elements and space planning are used in an interior environment. "An appropriately designed physical setting could be expected to evoke, or at least to serve as the focus of, a range of expected behaviors whose variations could be studied as a function not of physical parameters but of those complex social and psychological determinants that are rooted in all human activities and relationships" (Proshanky 173). Before providing a framework for design elements that define centrifugal and centripetal spaces, psychological reactions to spatial definitions have to be analyzed to anticipate one's reaction in a space.

Ingrained, learned reactions to a space can easily be described by one's interaction with a retail environment, a space nearly every person encounters. Observed during a study from the 1960s, "simply by the way [an environment] positions its hours, displays its merchandise, and situates its vendors, even a corner newsstand determines that business will be transacted in a predictable way" (Gallagher 128). Individuals know how to navigate through a store and what functions should be performed without much guidance, as is true with many public spaces. The spatial orientation of retail has been engrained into society to illicit a certain pattern of social interaction.

In analyzing social interaction, "spatial organization is measured in terms of physical and functional distance between persons, groups, and activities" (Gutman 97). Proshanky uses the terminology "sociofugal" and "sociopetal" to describe environments that encourage interaction and that discourage interaction (18). Sociofugal spaces include waiting rooms, while sociopetal spaces would be an old soda shop counter or a French sidewalk café (18). Proshanky conducted an experiment in a hospital cafeteria to see what type of table arrangement would be more conducive to a sociofugal environment versus a sociopetal environment. His team placed a variety of tables that sat two, four, or six individuals in a random arrangement throughout the cafeteria. The team observed that individuals preferred to sit at the larger tables, even if only two individuals were together.

Proshanky concluded, "Across-the-corner-at-right-angles is condusive only to: (a) conversations of certain types between (b) persons in certain relationships and (c) in very restricted cultural settings" (20). Individuals prefer to sit directly beside one another to have a conversation rather than across from one another. "In order for certain (behavioral cues) to be communicated successfully, people must be located in particular (measured) degrees of proximity to each other" (Gutman 100). The physical proximity of individuals and individuals' body language, positioned towards one another versus positioned away from one another, unconsciously convey an interest or disinterest in associating with one another.

Wells conducted a behavioral study to monitor the relationships in a large office. He surveyed employees that worked in two different office settings, all within the same company. The first group worked in a large, open area that encouraged collaboration. The second group worked in small areas but still collaborated on tasks. In the survey,

Wells asked the groups to name whom they would prefer to work with in the office. He found that preferences were directly related to distances between employees. Wells concluded that "internal group cohesion in the smaller areas was greater than in the open plan sections, even though the smaller areas included more isolates and had fewer links with those outside the smaller area" (Gutman 98). His study was conducted to determine how well large, open spaces that allow daylight and an outside view function as a collaborative environment (98). Wells's study indicates that a large, open area may not be as collaborative as current office trends imply. Large groups can also lead to behavioral issues with groups of children (Salyer). The intimacy of a smaller group is less overwhelming and provides an opportunity for personal relationships.

## DESIGN ELEMENTS

Another element of spatial orientation involves design elements that define space, including walls and geometric volumes. Enclosed spaces convey a sense of separation and containment (Rengel 60). Containment spaces have the ability to gather people and objects. Seen in design as a single wall, L-shaped planes, or U-shaped planes, contained spaces "translate into a sense of grounding and protection" while appealing to a need for security (60). Containment spaces do not necessarily form a barrier to adjacent spaces or completely enclose a space. Encapsulated spaces, on the other hand, do limit the connection between adjacent spaces. Doors can create an established path to enter, exit, and/or experience the space (60). Not only used in encapsulated spaces, door placement, as well as the arrangement of rooms, walls, and partitions, affect "the opportunities people have to see and hear each other and thus to respond to one another" (Gutman 97). Furthermore, "the location of barriers, apertures, and paths" can encourage communication or hinder it (97). The number of entry points into a room will further dictate whether or not communication is encouraged. A room with multiple entrances and exits encourages a communal relationship, while a space with only one entrance and exit relays an image of privacy (100). Ceiling planes can also be used to create a sense of enclosure. Lower ceiling planes enhance the intimacy of an environment. Ostentatiously high ceilings can also discourage interaction by making an individual feel lost in the space.

Geometries commonly used in design also carry psychological implications. Square spaces are "pure, formal, and static" (Rengel 70). Squares are generally spaces that house a specific function and are meant to be occupied. Because a square has four sides, it conveys a strong sense of enclosure and centrality (70). A circular space is also "pure, formal, and static" (70). Its rounded sides create a memorable shape with a strong center. The surrounding qualities of a circle also create a "strong sense of containment and enclosure" (70). Rectangular shapes can be either short, a ratio of less than 2:1 when comparing the longer and shorter sides, or long, a ratio greater than 2:1 when comparing the longer and shorter sides. Short rectangles convey a "strong sense of place," while long rectangles are more dynamic (70). The final shape is triangular. Triangles present a unique problem with small acute angles creating unusable space. Triangular spaces have the potential to make an impact and can be memorable when kept in pure proportions (71).

## APPLICATION FOR CENTRIFUGAL DESIGN

Centrifugal design can be equated to an extrovert, "one whose personality is gregarious and unreserved" ("Centrifugal"). Individuals' emotional reactions to centrifugal spaces should include high levels of arousal and pleasure, which encourage activity and interaction between individuals. Colors applied in a centrifugal space should be warmer like red, orange, and yellow. Cooler colors, like blue, green, and purple, can be used but should be used at high saturation levels to promote activity. Similarly, warm light should be used to encourage positive attitudes and activity. Warm light can be achieved through natural lighting or choosing lamps that have a lower color temperature.

Spatial arrangement of furniture should be conducive to conversation. Chairs should be arranged so individuals can sit side-by-side to have conversations instead of conversing across a table or space. The absence of walls and planes can also encourage involvement with the environment and other individuals, but the space should still be contained. Large open spaces can have the opposite effect desired in centrifugal design in making an individual to feel insecure and exposed. Thoughtfully placed L-shaped and U-shaped planes can help alleviate this problem. If the overall environment allows, space should be segmented to provide smaller group settings that allow for interaction or collaboration among individuals without an expansive void of space.

The use of horizontal lines and vertical lines also increases the energy in a space. Horizontal lines can signify movement and connection but can also provide a calming effect. Horizontal lines are often found in areas where individuals may experience anxiety, like a doctor's waiting room. Vertical lines, on the other hand, can contribute excitement and energy (Gore). A symbol of power, vertical lines can provide the illusion of height. As lines become thicker and bolder, the more noticeable their psychological effect becomes. A thin line may go undetected, while a wide line in a noticeable color will make an impact.

## APPLICATION FOR CENTRIPETAL DESIGN

Centripetal design focuses on inward attention and can be related to an introvert, "a shy or reserved person" ("Centripetal"). The introverted nature of centripetal design is applicable to individuals or groups of two to four individuals. In centripetal spaces, individuals' emotional response should be low levels of arousal and high levels of dominance, which encourage focus on self and avoidance of others. Cooler colors like blue, green, and purple in moderate to low saturation levels should be used to encourage introspection and relaxation. Warmer, generally more stimulating colors like red, orange, and yellow may also be used but with low saturation levels. Lighting should be cooler, as well. Although natural lighting is considered warm light, it may be used if adequately controlled and limited. Caution should be exercised to ensure that cool color lighting does not become sterile or agitating.

Spatial arrangement should convey privacy by enclosing and containing spaces. In centripetal spaces, boisterous conversation should not be encouraged. Chairs in areas provided for seclusion, if required to be in close proximity, should not be positioned to encourage conversation. This effect can be achieved by placing chairs back-to-back or directly across from one another. Limited conversation can also be achieved by placing seating areas far enough apart that conversation would be difficult for more than a few people gathered together. Use of large volumes and limited connections between spaces will also encourage only limited interaction among individuals. Volumes or spaces that are centralized or collected around a centermost space can also create an inward and central focus (Gore).

CONCLUSION

By recognizing the various psychological effects of color, light, and spatial orientation, designers can create spaces that encourage interaction, centrifugal design, or encourage inward focus, centripetal design. Understanding the psychological and physiological reactions to color can aid in determining which color palette and what levels of saturation would be appropriate to use in a defined space. Likewise, the color hue, color temperature, and amount of illumination can cause various psychological and physiological reactions. Although the psychological impact of spatial orientation is more difficult to grasp, space planning and architectural elements can help foster communication or discourage it. Regardless, "each individual interprets and gives meaning to his environment, and to this extent the real differences among individuals and groups lie not in how they behave but in how they perceive" (Proshanky 174).

BIBLIOGRAPHY

Birren, Faber. *Light, Color, and Environment: A discussion of the Biological and Psychological Effects of Color, with Historical Data and Detailed Recommendations for the Use of Color in the Environment.* Rev. ed., New York: Van Nostrand Reinhold, 1982. Print.

Cleland, T.M. *The Munsell Color System: A Practical Description with Suggestions for Its Use Apple Painter,* n.p. n.d. Web. 16 Nov 2011.

"Centrifugal." *Merriam-Webster Dictionary.* 2008. Print.

"Centripetal." *Merriam-Webster Dictionary.* 2008. Print.

Fehrman, Kenneth R., and Cherie Fehrman. *Color: The Secret Influence.* Hoboken: Prentice Hall, 2000. Print.

Gallagher, Winifred. *The Power of Place: How Our Surroundings Shape Our Thoughts, Emotions, and Actions.* New York: Poseidon Press, 1993. Print.

Gore, Kelly. "Form and Shape." Lehew Hall, Franklin. Spring 2010. Lecture.

Gore, Kelly. "Spatial Organization." Lehew Hall, Franklin. Spring 2010. Lecture.

Gutman, Robert, ed. *People and Buildings.* New York: Basic Books, 1972. Print.

Holtzschue, Linda. *Understanding Color: An Introduction for Designers.* 3rd ed. Hoboken: John Wiley & Sons, 2006. Print.

Mahnke, Frank H. *Color, Environment, & Human Response: An Interdisciplinary Understanding of Color and its Use as a Beneficial Element in the Design of the Architectural Environment.* New York: Van Nostrand Reinhold, 1996. Print.

Marberry, Sara O., and Laurie Zagon. *The Power of Color: Creating Healthy Interior Spaces.* New York: John Wiley & Sons, 1995. Print.

Mehrabian, Albert. *Public Places and Private Spaces: The Psychology of Work, Play, and Living Environments.* New York: Basic Books, 1976. Print.

Proshanky, Harold M., William H. Ittelson, and Leanne G. Rivlin, ed. *Environmental Psychology: Man and His Physical Setting.* New York: Holt, Rinehart, and Winston, 1970. Print.

Rengel, Roberto J. *Shaping Interior Space.* 2nd ed. New York:

Fairchild Publications, 2007. Print.

Salyer, Katie.  Personal Interview.  5 Oct. 2011.

Valdez, Patricia, and Albert Mehrabian.  "Effects of Color on Emotion."
    *Journal of Experimental Psychology: General.*  123.4 (1994):
    394-409.  Print.

Winchip, Susan M., *Designing A Quality Lighting Environment.*  New
    York: Fairchild Publications, 2005.  Print.

Angela D. Lee is an associate professor in the Visual Communications Department at O'More College of Design as well as a member of the President's Society of Fellows and Scholars. In addition to teaching, she is also a freelance graphic designer and illustrator. She received a Bachelor of Fine Arts in Visual Communications at Belmont University, a Master of Arts in Communication at Austin Peay State University, and is a Master of Fine Arts candidate for Visual Art at Azusa Pacific University. Her work has been featured in exhibitions across the country such as Expressions of Faith Juried Show at George Fox University; Positive/Negative Juried Show at East Tennessee State University; In Part at Belmont University; and Sessions, a video installment, at Open Lot in Nashville, Tennessee. She is an active member in Christians in Visual Arts, College Art Association, and AIGA and is particularly interested in subject matter involving video art, ancestry and identity within the American South, and graphic design history.

# AM I THE SAME PERSON
## ON FACEBOOK THAT I AM IN "REAL LIFE?"

### REALITY AND TRUTH CONCERNING IMAGE IN SOCIAL MEDIA: AN ANALYSIS USING *SCREEN* BY JESSICA HELFAND

**ANGELA LEE**

*Adjunct Professor, Visual Communications*

THE TITLE OF THE BOOK *Screen* by Jessica Helfand, prominent graphic design author and student of design legend Paul Rand, points to several themes. First, the book *Screen* shares a title with a column of the same name. The essays collected in this book were all first published in the column of the same name between 1994 and 2001 in *Eye* Magazine. Rick Poynor, founding editor of *Eye*, and Helfand together conceived of the column as a way to explore the physical space of the screen. This concept of a screen as a "point of departure," or a portal to a different world of interaction, is most of the book. As stated in the foreword by Helfand, the screen could be "a filter; a frame; a lens; a stage; a mirror or a canvas; a window or a mask; a point of departure or an inescapable destination; a civilization unto itself" (xv).

Although this sounds like a broad subject for the book, it is somewhat misleading. Some of the essays do indeed concentrate on the idea of the physical space of the screens that were most important at the time of the publication of this book: the screens of the computer and the television. Of course, the book omits the ever-present smartphone screen from the conversation because it didn't exist at the time of writing. Other omissions include the effect of self-publishing media platforms on new media and visual culture, such as YouTube, Twitter, Tumblr, and Blogger. These omissions and the title aside, the book puts forth a set of ideas that can be loosely-based around the single theme of visual culture, specifically how changes in visual culture have changed social interaction, the perception of time and truth, and the responsibility of the artist or designer and of the viewer.

## SOCIAL INTERACTION

First, Helfand tackles the subjects of social interaction. In the reality of social interaction, the screen seems to have reduced us to a single image, series of images, or a video that serves to represent "us." From this digital representation, people are then asked to judge whether or not they would like to "be our friend" if we are on Facebook or MySpace, leave a comment if we are on YouTube, or otherwise draw a collective judgment against our image based on only a small window of who we are. We build this image sometimes from carefully selected pieces, other times from haphazard posts. Essentially, when we create this digital representation, we are creating a digital scarecrow for the field of screens. "Hype is hip, and pictures speak much, *much* louder than words," Helfand observes, before quoting playwright Sam Shepard, who says we'd rather "watch you on television than talk to you. Just get rid of you altogether and make you an image" (80). So, the screen seems to have reduced social interaction to a mere judgment of worth, a weighing of the scales to decide if my greedily consuming your image is actually worth the time investment (80).

The recent sexting scandal of Representative Weiner comes to mind. It is a dramatic example, but an excellent one. With the release of a single image to a single screen comes a host of responsibilities in the management of your electronic reputation. You had better make sure that each and every image viewed on a screen represents you in the way you wish to be represented. Surely Weiner's image represented him to a female friend the way he intended, but what he did not intend was for the world to draw a judgment on the same image. The lesson here is that with the release of each and every image to a screen, your reputation must be considered. The adage of only releasing electronic images that you would show to you mother certainly works here. Had Weiner applied this to his image selection, he would still have a job.

## REAL TIME, FAKE TIME, AND PRODUCTIVITY

The screen and the tools of screen interaction skew time. We are lured by the "seductive play of sensory choreography" of the screen into believing we are getting much more completed in the time that we have (Helfand 57). It is an illusion of productivity. The term "real time" has grown to imply an instantaneous sensory experience, with no waiting period. If "real time" means it happens instantly, then what does "fake time" do? Helfand says, "Real time, in this context, is a misnomer: a more worthy definition comes from cognitive psychologist Donald Norman, who rightly observes that 'real time is what humans do'" (4). If real time is the continuum along which humans actually exist, the time that exists when having a screen interaction is actually the fake one of the two time spaces.

## TRUTH

Mentioning the word "fake" brings us to the problem of truth within the space of the screen. There are different truths at stake within the screen environment. Rep. Weiner neglected the truth that he is a married man when deciding to use certain photos to craft his screen presence. Beyond this, we seem to be perfectly comfortable with creating simulations to place onto the screen, sidestepping reality all the way. This weird happenstance is made even stranger by the popularity of reality shows that (supposedly) show the truth. Many have been exposed as heavily edited into a contrived reality; they are not as real as they seem. As Helfand points out, despite living in the information era where "opportunities for information access grow more plentiful by the second, the opportunities for fact-finding, or truth-seeking, or knowledge building grow dimmer" (81). Like the "pseudo-events" she describes by Daniel Boorstein, in which synthetic situations, or a contrived reality, are replacing actuality, we live in a world where the description of the experience, or the spin-off media from something, can actually eclipse the reality of the event itself. We are satisfied with replacing the authentic with the synthetic (80-81).

## PERSONAL RESPONSIBILITY OF THE ARTIST

Where does this place the responsibility of the artist, when creating images, and of the viewer, when interpreting the images? The artist is charged with the responsibility of creating the visual cues that are then absorbed by the viewer. An artist can choose to manipulate the visual to "hook" the audience, taking the angle of truth, sensationalism, or a mix of the two in order to craft a story (Helfand 83). If the artist (or art director) is mixing reality with fiction to create a more compelling visual product, what are the ethical ramifications of releasing such a product into the marketplace? Cultivation theory, a theory of communication studies, dictates that we craft our idea of the world from exposure to what we see on television. If every newscast we see is about robbery and rape, for example, we believe the world is a much more dangerous and lewd place than it actually is. The stream of bad news on the screen becomes our reality, regardless of the facts. Could cultivation theory then be applied to the products of an artist or art director? If an artist is creating a visual that replaces reality for the viewer, how responsible should the artist be?

Then there is the problem of sound within these visual products. As I've discovered in my own work, keeping the balance of sound against the visual can be quite challenging. Helfand feels the same way about sound, saying that it "interrupts interpretation" and can end up driving the design at hand. It short-circuits the conversation that the viewer can have with the visual, "telegraph[ing] the ending" and stopping the viewers from injecting their own experience into the work of art (127). In other words, sometimes the absence of sound is the only sound that is needed in a work of art. As Helfand states, the "silence is deafening" (129).

## THE NEW ILLITERACY

So where does the responsibility of the viewer lie within the interpretation of the visual? Helfand does not answer this question directly, but instead explores what she refers to as the creation of a "new illiteracy" within the viewership. This new illiteracy is driven by the tendency of the viewer to select only information that serves the need to achieve the "most radical forms of individualism and the most intriguing means of social interaction" (93). In a society where anyone can use the magic of a screen to "do, say, be anything," basic principles like the ability to use "good sentence structure, editing techniques, or the ability to articulate an original idea" have lost their value (93). The new illiteracy, then, embraces the filtering of ideas for selfish reasons.

Recently, the Cheekwood Museum in Nashville showcased several works by the abstract expressionists from the Smithsonian. I visited the show on more than one occasion and heard the same comments each time. "My first grader could have painted this." "That just looks like a bunch of scribbles to me." Similar comments abounded. Instead of the show placing a responsibility on the viewer for education related to the historical art movement represented, the viewers were instead expecting the work to conform to their visual standards. Instead of feeling dumb, these people were voicing their ignorance of the works represented out loud and sans shame. This represents the new illiteracy quite well, albeit without the use of a screen. With the plethora of online choices, it is very easy to visually cherry-pick your way through images, selecting only those that best represent how you see yourself, ignorant of the historical meaning attached to each image.

## THE CHARGE OF SOCIAL RESPONSIBILITY TO DESIGNERS

John Maeda frames Helfand's thoughts in the introduction, stating that the only hope for the discipline of design to survive the splintering of visual culture will be "a salvation based upon strong personal voices" (xx-xxi). It seems that aligning with these voices will need to be an ethical and controlled approach to creating socially responsible works. The viewer must be allowed freedom of interpretation when considering the visual, whether we agree with the interpretation or not. We must also be aware of the ethical considerations of how we are manipulating the visual situation and how we are affecting the outcome for the viewer.

## REFERENCES

Helfand, Jessica. *Screen: Essays on Graphic Design, New Media, and Visual Culture.* New York: Princeton Architectural Press, 2001. Print.

Joshua Lomelino, Associate Professor and Department Chair of the Visual Communications Department at O'More College of Design, has three degrees: an M.F.A. from Savannah College of Art and Design, an M.A. from Savannah College of Art and Design, and a B.S. from Illinois State University. He is a member of the President's Society of Fellows and Scholars. Lomelino owns and operates Anomaly Studios, a design firm specializing in graphic design, interactive design, and animation. He is a member of the Golden Key International Society and is an award-winning animator. Lomelino's past projects include work in the areas of interactive design, animated films, 3D product visualization, 3D special effects, game development, and programming. He is the co-author and animator of the children's animated movie *In the Beginning There Were Dinosaurs*, author of *Animation School*, and developer of several learning-management technologies which are used internationally by colleges and universities.

# Discovery Island –
## An Interactive Game-Based Educational Environment

### JOSHUA LOMELINO
*Associate Professor*
*Chair, Visual Communications*

THIS ARTICLE discusses the creation of my M.F.A. thesis for the Savannah College of Art and Design. While the documentation here is a preview of sorts, I hope to at least provide a snapshot of the type of research and work I did to create a fully-functional set of interactive game worlds.

My thesis focused on the development of interactive learning games for children, teaching language arts and math concepts through interactive learning activities on a location called Discovery Island. The written component focuses on the challenges of creating developmentally-appropriate interactive activities in digital game-based learning, where the visual component illustrated the development of game-based learning tools that attempt to promote effective solutions for interactive challenges. The focus of the game development was to create a game environment that was infused with perceptive programming logic that adapts to the learners' skills and knowledge levels in the pursuit of a developmentally-aware, game-based learning environment.

My theory was that digital gaming could be utilized not only as a tool for reinforcement and as a teaching aid, but also as a primary teaching tool for pre-school and kindergarten-age students.

The visual component of the thesis is Discovery Island, a fully-functional game that illustrates how gradated levels, learning difficulty levels, in conjunction with a guided assistance algorithm, can not only teach students, but may also help and encourage students' learning into higher developmental levels (difficulty levels). An intelligent teaching and learning system is one that does not go from easy to difficult, but gradually adapts to the child's skill level and consistently monitors his or her progress and performance. Coaching and assistance are provided at easier levels, and as the children "level up," they perform more independently with more advanced challenges.

The written component of my thesis describes the process of the project development. This paper discusses my research of educational theory, to user testing, to production. The thesis weaves together theory and practice and shows the genesis of Discovery Island through to its conclusion. It also discusses how the target audience interacted and responded to the game environment through user testing.

This overview document is a snapshot of a much longer and detailed research endeavor in the form of a thesis. The purpose of this overview is to hint at the overall concepts. Also, the visual component is meant to fully embody the concepts discussed in the research component. You may play the fully functional game online by visiting http://www.anomalystudios.com and clicking through to the products section. Following are short excerpts from the thesis document.

## EDUCATIONAL METHODOLOGIES APPLIED TO DISCOVERY ISLAND

The learning process is complex and multidimensional. It is a difficult phenomenon to describe in simplified formulaic terms. Over the years there have been theories presented (some more widely accepted than others) that attempt to describe how learning takes place. What we are left with today after centuries of debate from people ranging from Confucius to Plato to Dewey are a collection of ideas—or theories with regard to how people learn and the nuances in the educational process (Palmer). In this section I will discuss various educational methodologies, synthesized and adapted from theorists and cognitive psychologists. While this is not a paper on educational methodologies, I feel it is important to discuss how the game's methodology was developed and influenced by some of the pioneers in educational methodology and theory.

In the field of pedagogical study there are varying perspectives and attitudes regarding how theories of education play out in traditional education as well as digital game-based learning. Each vantage point dissects the teaching and learning process from a different angle, but there is one commonality amongst the various opinions: they view the learner in relation to skills, knowledge, and experiences, where the learner is a unique individual, and not a generalized numerical statistic. Throughout this paper educational methodology theories will be presented in conjunction with the design methodology of Discovery Island. In this way I will show how design decisions were based on my methodology "best practices" research.

Digital game-based learning provides a number of advantages to learners, and in many ways they do so by drawing on discoveries made in traditional learning environments. Because of this I felt it was important to start my game development by first analyzing strategies used in the classroom and home environments in teaching pre-school and kindergarten-age students. In developing the methodological procedures for Discovery Island, I started by analyzing the learning objectives in kindergarten classrooms. This naturally led to various learning activities (such as activity pages and other physically-based learning activities) that are conducted in kindergarten classrooms. Since I was creating an interactive approach to learning it was important to work through foundational voices who supported the notion of "learning by doing." This led me to the works of John Dewey, Maria Montessori, Erik Erikson, Jean Piaget, Lev Vygotsky, and others.

While each viewpoint on the educational and learning process varies on many points, the one common thread between each voice is that the learner is a unique individual with a unique learning pace. To put it metaphorically, learners are like snowflakes. Each child brings a unique set of challenges to the teaching process.

The primary challenge in developing a game environment that is intended to be used for learning is that there are a myriad of educational design concerns to consider and process. It was therefore helpful to have as a basis of comparison, voices of authority to compare my learning environment against for validation. Perhaps one of the most notable voices is that of John Dewey. In his book *How Computer Games Help Children Learn*, David Shaffer discusses Dewey's influential work in education. He relates how Dewey's groundbreaking school was developed:

> John Dewey founded the Chicago Laboratory School in
> 1896 as a response to problems he saw in the industrial
> school system that had been developed in the United

States in the last half of the nineteenth century. By 1904 the school was the most innovative experiment in education in the country, and the ideas of progressive education Dewey explored there would inspire educational innovation, policy, and theory for the next century. (Shaffer 124)

The educational practices of "learning by doing," as I will discuss later in this paper, can largely be attributed to John Dewey. Dewey's contributions to the field of education, and even to digital game-based learning, are helpful and influential. One of his ideas was that learning activities need to have clear organization and purpose. "Dewey believed that an activity is not a learning activity if it lacks purpose and organization" (Mooney 14). While applying these findings to my thesis project development, I found these thoughts challenging and life-giving throughout the production of Discovery Island. In many ways this became a catalyst for implementing a thoughtful approach to the organization and purpose of each learning activity.

As a result, the design approach for Discovery Island became centered on the objective of providing organization and purpose for learning activities. The organization for the learning environment is facilitated across several island locations. Each island focuses on specific spheres of skills and knowledge bases. The island locations for my game that facilitate the organized learning activities are

- Word Center
- Counting Cave
- Shapes Mountain
- Singing Forest.

Each location was designed to aid in the development of math and language arts skills. In this way my aim was to create learning activities that were simulations of the teaching methodologies used in the "real world."

Carol Mooney goes on to synthesize the thoughts, writings, and ideas of John Dewey and helped further the organization and purpose of my learning activities. She summarizes that "from Dewey's perspective, an experience can only be called educational if it meets these criteria:

- it is based on the children's interests and grows out of their existing knowledge and experience

- it supports the children's development
- it helps the children develop new skills
- it adds to the children's understanding of their world
- it prepares the children to live more fully" (Mooney 14).

In this fashion Discovery Island draws on the "best practices" from teachers and their methods used in and out of the classroom. Each island location attempts to provide learning activities based on a child's interests and then grow out of these existing spheres of knowledge and experience, while attempting to support his or her development of new skills.

## CHILD-CENTERED ENVIRONMENTS

*The greatest sign of success for a teacher is to be able to say, "the children are now working as if I did not exist." Maria Montessori* (qtd. in Mooney 23)

Another central figure who has helped shape the climate and culture of learning for many children and teachers, both past and present, is Maria Montessori. Maria was an educator who has had a far-reaching impact in the practices and strategies of education. She has been an inspiration for my work in creating Discovery Island as I analyzed and developed strategies for implementing a child-centered learning environment. She was trained as a scientist, and this background laid the foundation for the success of her work. She is known for her great success in teaching the "unteachable." She used observation to determine the unique needs of children and developed strategies based off these observations (Mooney 22). It was in her early years developing the Children's House (for children in impoverished conditions) that her teaching and learning strategies were created. A unique approach was needed for her group of learners, and, out of the unique needs, a unique solution was born.

"Montessori acknowledged that the emphasis she placed on preparation of the environment was probably the main characteristic by which people identified her method" (Mooney 24). She believed that children learn best through sensory experiences. She thought that the teacher has a responsibility to provide wonderful sights, textures, sounds, and smells for children. The more senses that can be incorporated into each learning experience, the greater the opportunity for impact and retention.

Discovery Island attempts to implement a digital game-based solution for the types of learning interactions that are possible in the real-world. While there are limitations that a computer-based environment imposes on sensory learning, my goal was to create a child-centered environment in the visual design (visual learning), audio design (audible learning), and interaction design (haptic/kinesthetic learning). This attempts to emulate one-on-one tutoring. Realizing that many children have limited mouse skills at this age, the personal interactions were designed to be playable by children, even those with limited computer skills.

## LEARNING THROUGH EXPLORATION

*"I never try to teach my students anything. I only try to create an environment in which they can learn."* Albert Einstein (qtd. in Prensky 71)

Another guiding factor in the development of Discovery Island was that of learning through exploration. Instead of children passively learning facts and information in a pre-set linear format, my approach to teaching and learning is more non-linear and requires exploration as children attempt to find correct solutions. Montessori provided insight into this notion of exploration as a means of learning. She believed that exploration and repetition were components to successful student engagement and learning. Discovery Island unites and marries together the concepts of exploration and repetition in areas such as the Word Center and Shapes Mountain where students visualize and attempt word and letter combinations and identify shapes and geometric forms. Mooney speaks into the work of Montessori in the areas of exploration and repetition. She goes on to say that

> Montessori believed that children learn best by doing, and through repetition. She thought they did things over and over to make an experience their own, as well as to develop skills. Montessori urged teachers not to interfere with the child's patterns and pace learning. She thought it was the teacher's job to prepare the environment, provide appropriate materials, and then step back and allow the children the time and space to experiment. Open-ended

scheduling, with large blocks of time for free work and play,
is part of Montessori's legacy. (Mooney 29)

The foundation of Discovery Island was constructed in such a way that children can both explore and learn at the same time in a unified fashion. In this way the game design element of interaction was centered around the pedagogical element of repetition. The Word Center and Singing Forest, for example, allow for over a hundred words that children can progress through in various difficulty levels as they are guided to the correct answers. I like to think of this as learning through immersion where they learn through exploration and by doing.

Among the list of theorists who can speak on learning through exploration, Piaget offers many helpful theories into methodological approaches for digital game-based learning. Piaget is known for his stages of cognitive development theory and is a psychologist that offers insights into how children arrive at their knowledge base (Mooney 60). His ideas helped establish precedence for the notion of learning through exploration.

Carol Mooney discusses the work of Piaget and states that "while others asked what children know or when they know it, Piaget asked how children arrive at what they know" (Mooney 60). This is important for learning game environments because of their non-linear fashion. By developing multiple paths and opportunities for discovery, the art of teaching and learning may be made more effective in the digital game environment. Mooney goes on to say that children's interactions with their environment are what create learning. She discusses the work of Piaget in the context of exploration and how children "construct their own knowledge by giving meaning to the people, places, and things in their world" (Mooney 61). Piaget was fond of the expression "construction is superior to instruction" (Mooney 62). This became a foundational element for the Word Center portion of my game development as I grappled with the ways to facilitate and support children's skills in learning how to construct words using word families in conjunction with phonetic pronunciation cues.

Another important contribution to my design process came from Piaget, who like Dewey, "believed that children learn only when their curiosity is not fully satisfied. He thought that children's curiosity actually drives their learning" (Mooney 60-62). This summarizes the concepts and ideas of "learning through exploration." In this fashion— learning through exploration— the game design approach allows children to explore the many elements of each island location in a non-linear fashion. They are allowed to explore new locations while building their skills and increasing their knowledge.

## ACTIVE LEARNING

In the area of child-centered learning environments, Lev Vygotsky offers valuable insight into potential best practices for active learning. Vygotsky was a literature teacher who became interested in cognitive and language development and was keenly interested in how people learn (Mooney 81). Vygotsky also offers meaningful insight for how people learn. Vygotsky believed that education should be an active exchange with the learner. Instead of viewing the educational experience as a static flow or stream from teacher to student, Vygotsky believed that people were active participants in the learning process. Mooney states that "as a progressive educator he shared with Vygotsky, Montessori, and Piaget the central ideas of that movement: education must be both active and interactive" (Mooney 83).

Naturally, in interactive learning environments, the possibilities for active and interactive learning are abundant. In my game development I employed the use of audio, images, sounds, and interactivity to help create a fully immersive interactive experience for learners. In this fashion, my intent was to create an environment where active learning could take place.

A precept of active learning is that actions taken by learners are met with resistance. This is a key to the effectiveness of active learning. If an action encounters resistance, the natural response is for the learner to push harder, either out of his or her own volition or through other means. David Shaffer, an author on game theory and practice, offers up his thoughts on obstacles, and I feel this is a crucial element of the game design that Discovery Island incorporates with its levels of difficulty and number of tries design:

> Dewey's point is an important one, and the center of
> any progressive view of education: We learn by trying
> to accomplish some goal in the face of obstacles. When
> we bump into an obstacle, we have to step back and try

to figure out what we know—and what else we need to know—to help us get past it. Of course, if there is nothing we are trying to do, then when we bump into an obstacle, we just give up, which is why we have to be doing something we care about. (Shaffer 125)

In this fashion, active learning requires obstacles to overcome, and provides the impetus for children to continue playing in order to overcome these obstacles.

## LEARNING BY DOING AND LEARNING THROUGH PLAY

Play is a profound element in the learning process—and for game development the element of play is a natural fit. "If you listen closely to children (particularly preschool and elementary school children) talk about their pretend play, they use the word game for all kinds of activities that are collaborative, ongoing, and have nothing to do with what we would consider winning in the traditional sense: 'Let's play The Firefighter's Game': 'Let's play The Superhero Game': 'Let's Play House' (Shaffer 22). The concept of play is a natural extension to the active and powerful imaginations of young children.

## FUN AND LEARNING

Perhaps one of the most challenging game elements to accomplish while attempting to achieve educational goals is the element of fun. There is challenging balance between the content, the way it is presented, and how the content and gameplay is intertwined to facilitate fun and learning. "Piaget stressed the importance of play as an important avenue for learning" (Mooney 62). In the real world children learn by play, and fun opens up many pathways of discovery.

Clark Aldrich talks about fun as a game design element in his book *Learning by Doing*. He laments on the topic when he discusses the challenging aspects of fun. He says in one concise sentence that "fun gives me a lot of unhappiness" (149). He then goes on to say that "fun is a very difficult concept for educational simulation designers. First, and this goes without saying, is that computer games are meant to be fun. They are designed to be fun" (Aldrich 149). This is a very challenging notion and is one that is quite difficult to accomplish. In Discovery Island I tried to implement the element of fun through the visual design elements, the audio, and the interactivity. In the Counting Cave for example, a narrative is established that animals have escaped from a cave, and the children are asked if they can help the animals get back into the cave by dragging them into the cave. In this fashion the game attempts to be the scaffolding for the learners.

## SCAFFOLDING AND INTERACTIVE SIMULATIONS

The pioneers in progressive education that I have referenced present to us a unique set of challenges when evaluating digital gaming as a mode of teaching, learning, and reinforcement. When digital gaming is used as a means to simulate experiences in the pursuit of teaching and learning, there are many factors that should be considered.

One such factor is the consideration of the role of the computer and game design in the process of teaching and learning.

Vygotsky referred to the assistance a teacher or peer offers a child as *scaffolding*. A house painter working on a house uses a scaffold to reach parts of the house that would otherwise be out of reach. In the same way, adults and peers can help a child 'reach' a new concept or skill by giving supporting information. Vygotsky believed this could be done not only by the teacher but also by the child's peers who already possess the desired skills. (Mooney 28)

Discovery Island was designed to act as the "scaffolding" for children as they learn and interact in the digital environment. Its design mirrors what can be done in the real world and simulates how teaching and learning may be conducted.

The game design approach for Discovery Island was to create an environment where the role of the teacher could be simulated through audio and visual guidance, coupled with the child's interactions. Discovery Island, from a standpoint of computer theory, is a "microworld." A microworld is a simulated world, wholly contained in a digital environment that can provide a scaffolding for the learning process. David Shaffer provides valuable insight into the concept of a microworld in conjunction with learning:

> Learning to use a computer means learning to work with simulations because every computer program is a simulation: it represents some part of the world—real or

imagined—and bits of code in memory area the program moves those bits around in ways that we can use to tell us something about the real or imagined world on which the simulation is based. Every computer program creates a world: what Seymour Papert and others have called a *microworld*. A microworld is a little universe we can explore—and a universe that, like the one we inhabit with our physical bodies responds differently depending on what we do with it. (Shaffer 67)

In this fashion, Discovery Island is a microworld that serves as scaffolding in the active learning process. The goal of each island location's design is to help enhance learning, where learners embrace multiple stimuli at once—from interactivity to content and other stimuli in a concurrent fashion.

Thinking about games solely as simulation, however, can be a somewhat limited view of the full potential for creating learning moments. "Rather than thinking about *games* and *simulation*, it is more productive to think about the distinct elements, namely:

- *Simulation* elements
- *Game* elements
- *Pedagogical* elements" (Aldrich 80-81).

The challenge in creating the right blend of simulation, game design, and pedagogical elements is to establish an effective balance and proportion for each of these ingredients. Aldrich goes on to say that "simulation elements selectively represent objects or situations, and selectively represent user interaction. Simulation elements enable discovery, experimentation, role modeling, practice, and active construction of systems, cyclical, and linear content" (Aldrich 81).

In this sense, simulation does not become the sole method of explaining the full potential of learning that can take place in a digital game-based environment. Instead, simulation is blended together with the game elements and pedagogical elements to create the overall mix in the gameplay experience.

SUMMARY

The voices of Dewey, Montessori, Eriskon, Piaget, and Vygotsky, among others, help make sense and bring order and structure to the challenges of teaching young children. While their foundational work was done some time ago, around the early 1900s, the impact of their work is still felt and resonates today in teaching methods and strategies. Their thoughts helped develop strategies for digital game-based learning methods as well.

Integrating the principles of their discoveries in the field of teaching and learning into my game environment helped structure and format the game to be a place where children could be coached and guided through the learning process.

The remainder of the thesis discusses the specific game design and visual design techniques and practices that were used to embody a game environment that utilized the abovementioned educational theories and practices. To view the game in more detail and to see it in action please visit http://www.anomalystudios.com and click through to the educational products section.

WORKS CITED

Aldrich, Clark. *Learning by Doing*. Pfeiffer & Co, 2005. Print.

Eston, Rebeka and Shulman, Linda. *Growing Mathematical Ideas in Kindergarten*. Math Solutions, 1999. Print.

Mooney, Carol. *Theories of Childhood*. Redleaf Pr, 2000. Print.

Palmer, Joy, Liora Bresler, David Cooper. *Fifty Major Thinkers on Education. Routledge,* 2001. Print.

Shaffer, David, and James Gee. *How Computer Games Help Children Learn*. Palgrave MacMillan, 2008. Print.

Prensky, Marc. *Digital Game-Based Learning*. Paragon House Publishers, 2007. Print.

Prensky, Marc. *Don't Bother Me Mom I'm Learning*. Burns & Oates, 2006. Print.

BIBLIOGRAPHY

Allphin, Lawren. "Reading: What Happens in the First Few Months of Kindergarten?" *Education*. Web. 14 Sept. 2009.


Allphin, Lawren. "Math: What Happens in the First Few Months of Kindergarten?" *Education*. Web. 14 Sept. 2009.

"Grade-by-Grade Learning: Kindergarten." *PBS Parents*. Web. 14 Sept. 2009.

Graham, Judith. "Brain Development: What We Know About How Children Learn". *University of Maine- Family Issue Facts*. Web. 14 Sept. 2009.

Katz, Lilian G. "What Should Be Learned In Kindergarten?" *KidSource*. February 1994. Web.14 Sept 2009.

Moats, Louisa. "How Children Learn to Spell." *Scholastic*. Web. 25 Sept. 2009.

Perrone, Vito. "Mathematics in Kindergaten". *Family Education*. Web. 14 Sept. 2009.

Roussou, Maria. "Learning by Doing and Learning Through Play: AnExploration of Interactivity in Virtual Environments for Children." *ACM Portal*. January 2004. Web. 25 Sept. 2009.

"What do Students Learn in Kindergarten Language Arts?" *WorksheetLibrary*. Web. 14 Sept. 2009.

"Word Families." *Enchanted Learning*. Web. 14 Sept. 2009.

Associate Professor Jessa R. Sexton has been teaching at O'More College of Design since 2006. Her other roles at the College include serving as Executive Editor of O'More Publishing and Director of the Hilliard Institute for Educational Wellness. She also directs students involved in the Townsend Institute for Global Competency and is a member of the President's Society of Fellows and Scholars. In June of 2007, she explored Oxford, England, where she was a visiting fellow of Harris Manchester College. Published author of two text books and two children's books, her latest writing and research endeavors include color symbolism and further study into the life and works of one of her favorite authors, Ernest Hemingway.

# HEMINGWAY – LADIES' MAN?

### JESSA R. SEXTON
*Associate Director, Hilliard Institute for Educational Wellness*
*Associate Professor, Liberal Arts*

PERHAPS EVEN GREATER KNOWN than his fiction is Hemingway himself. Because of his boundless reputation, readers and critics alike often associate themes, events, and characters in Hemingway's works to the author's life. Carlos Baker, one of the first and often noted as the most thorough of Hemingway's biographers, does not believe that such associations are inherently wrong. In his article entitled "A Search for the Man as He Really Was," Baker explains the natural connection between Hemingway and his fiction as such:

> A third source of biographical data which must be treated with more than usual circumspection is Hemingway's fiction itself. One important plank in his esthetic platform [was] the writer's obligation to tell the truth. This meant, in fictional practice, that he seldom wanted to depart very far from events in which he had played some personal part.

Of course some have taken it too far, assuming that every word read is dripping with Hemingway's biography. Some critics even take the words of Hemingway's characters and quote them as words from the mouth of Hemingway, a close relative, or friend. Still, Carlos Baker's statement holds a level of truth. A writer cannot detach his own experiences and relationship from his writing without veering from "the writer's obligation to tell the truth." Hemingway's beliefs, as well as his personal connections with people, are revealed in his works. Particularly of interest to many critics is how Hemingway's works connect with his views about women. In some of his short fiction, Hemingway reflects his own relationships with women through his female characters by showing their manipulation of, manipulation by, or worthlessness to male characters.

## THE MANIPULATIVE WOMAN

*In His World*

One of the more popular stereotypical Hemingway female characters is no better described than as the manipulative, controlling b-word. In his own life, Hemingway experiences such pressures from dominating women. In *Ernest Hemingway: A Life Story*, Carlos Baker describes Hemingway's mother, Grace, as having dressed him just as his sister. "At the age of nine months he had his picture taken in a pink gingham dress and a wide hat ornamented with flowers" (3). The woman even called her little boy "Ernestine" ("Ernest Hemingway Biography and Notes"). Mrs. Hemingway was not catering to her son's natural feminine nature. If anything she was stifling him and perhaps pressing him to overcome these things by exerting himself as a man. Baker illustrates this notion when he describes Hemingway as a boy:

> His aspiration was to be taken for a man. He stomped about with half an old musket on his shoulder. He memorized some stanzas from Tennyson's 'Charge of the Light Brigade' and became forthwith a soldier, gathering various pieces of wood which he called his blunderbuss, his shotgun, his rifle, his Winchester, and his pistol. (5)

Later in life, Hemingway found himself caught up in a relationship with a different kind of manipulative woman. Agnes Von Kurowsky was Hemingway's first experience in love. Though the nurse doted on him during his stay in a Milan hospital, he was not the only admirer who received her affections. Though Baker explains that Agnes did not let their relationship evolve physically beyond kissing, she did lead him on to a deep emotional level. Agnes did not desire to settle down or get married, which were the intentions of young Hemingway. Baker describes Agnes as such: "she recognized the need of some variety. The boys on the top floor all adored her. Sometimes she let them take her to dinner, as she had done with Captain Serena, and as she did with Henry Villard after his jaundice was cured" (50).

As Hemingway prepared to leave the hospital, though, it truly seemed that Agnes cared for only him. While they were apart, she wrote often, sometimes twice a day. Eventually, her letters appeared less frequently, and then the messages became less endearing. She once signed with affectionate terms of endearment; then her correspondence became less warm. "Anyone less in love than Ernest might have read the signs of approaching disaster between the lines of Agnes's letter" (Baker 59). In truth, Agnes had begun to love another. Baker writes that Hemingway "was beside himself with horror and dismay" (59).

Hemingway's mother and his first love were not the only women in his life who manipulated or controlled him. According to J. Gerald Kennedy and Kirk Curnutt of Louisiana State University, Gertrude Stein also used her persuasive power as a way to direct the young male author. The critics explain that "Stein initially treated Hemingway as a protégé and (according to *A Moveable Feast*) lectured him on money, food, clothing, art, literature, and sex" (3). At first, Hemingway accepted her influence as an aid and enjoyed her interest in his work and life. Later on, he did not as merrily welcome her persistent "blunt criticism" (3). Kennedy and Curnutt explain, "As he learned his craft and began to publish stories, however, he grew impatient with Stein's imperious manner and looked to establish his literary independence" (3). Kenneth Lynn even connects Stein to Grace Hemingway explicating that Hemingway was drawn to Stein as a replacement mother. Both women had an irresistible while at the same time frustrating habit of controlling young Ernest (qtd. in Kennedy and Curnutt 4).

In 1924, Hemingway used his own connections in the literary world to get Stein's narrative, *The Making of Americans*, published. He did much of the work preparing the manuscript for publication himself. This labor, Kennedy and Curnutt believe, was not one made entirely selflessly, but with a desire to pay back Stein for her help, a help that controlled his actions in getting her work published. "He carried out this labor, it would appear, less to promote Stein's work than to amass the necessary credit to cancel his own debt" (3). Hemingway's energies were expended in hopes of getting rid of the control he felt Stein had over him as long as he was indebted to her for all of her literary help.

### In His Work

Controlling and manipulative women are present in Hemingway's short stories as well. Kennedy and Curnutt's article about Stein, "Out of the Picture: Mrs. Krebs, Mother Stein, and 'Soldier's Home,'" explicitly makes the connection between Hemingway's life and his characters. Stein is said to have controlled some of Hemingway's professional actions, just as Mrs. Krebs in "Soldier's Home" tries to control and manipulate her son. The critics write, "What Krebs cannot make his mother see is that he is no longer her little boy; combat has changed him" (8). Indeed, Krebs's mother will not treat him like the adult he has become. When he comes in to the kitchen one morning, she scolds him like a little child, "Harold, please don't muss up the paper. Your father can't read his Star if it's been mussed" (Hemingway 149). Later, her actions become more and more depreciating as she pushes him to work, for "there can be no idle hands in His Kingdom . . . all work is honorable" (151), and lays several guilt trips on him: "I have prayed for you. I pray for you all day long, Harold . . . Don't you love your mother, dear boy?" (151). When he says no, probably out of angry for her treatment of him or confusion after life-changing events in the war, she uses woman's most cruel motivator: she cries. After another guilt trip from her, "I held you next to my heart when you were a tiny baby" (152), he finally completely gives in, signified by his calling her "Mummy" and kneeling with her as she prays for him (153). He stops thinking of his trauma from the war and plans to please his mother by fulfilling her wish for his employment. "He had felt sorry for his mother and she had made him lie. He would go to Kansas City and get a job and she would feel all right about it" (153). In the end, as Margaret D. Bauer describes it, "Krebs's mother bullies her son to shape up" (133).

Another short story in which Hemingway portrays a controlling woman is "The Short Happy Life of Francis Macomber." Margot Macomber's first actions in the story, "She did not speak to him [her husband] when she came in" gives the first hint to her icy nature (5). When she does speak, she makes every effort to dominate the conversation at hand. "Margaret, his wife, looked away from him and back to Wilson. 'Let's not talk about the lion,' she said" (5). Whether or not she knows that her husband's triumph in his safari hunt was actually a failure, the point remains that Margot is not interested in talking about her husband; she is interested in talking to Wilson. When she later remarks that "conversation is going to be so difficult," she feels so because she knows that talking about her husband will be unavoidable after his incident with the lion (5). When things do not go her way in the conversation, she begins to cry and leaves the men alone.

Wilson very quickly identifies this sort of woman, having known many of her type from all of the hunting expeditions he has guided. He describes her kind as such: "They are, he thought, the hardest in the world; the hardest, the cruelest, the most predatory and the most attractive and their men have softened or gone to pieces nervously as they have hardened. Or is it that they pick men they can handle?" (Hemingway 8). When Margot comes back and announces that she will join them on tomorrow's hunt, "'I'm coming,' she said. 'No, you're not.' 'Oh, yes, I am. Mayn't I, Francis?' 'Why not stay in camp?' 'Not for anything,' she said. 'I wouldn't miss something like today for anything,'" Wilson further reflects, "she is away for twenty minutes and now she is back, simply enameled in that American female cruelty. They are the damnedest women. Really the damnedest . . . She's damn cruel but they're all cruel. They govern, of course, and to govern one has to be cruel sometimes. Still, I've seen enough of their damn terrorism" (9, 10). Wilson persists in telling her she cannot come, but she replies, "You're very mistaken" (9).

Margot is not a woman who is used to being told what to do. Wilson's description of Margot's and Francis's relationship, that the wife has picked a man she could "handle," fits the situation perfectly. In the end, when Margot notices her husband maturing from one of the "great American boy-men" into an actual man, she takes a drastic measure. "Mrs. Macomber, in the car, had shot at the buffalo with the 6.5 Mannlicher as it seemed about to gore Macomber and had hit her husband about two inches up and a little to one side of the base of his skull" (36). Wilson, as intuitive as ever, notices her intentions. "He *would* have left you too," he reminds her (36). Margot knows her husband is no longer a man she could control, so she kills him.

Critic Susan K. Harris describes Margot as "a destroyer in the first person—first of her husband's potency, then of his life" (78). She explains that though Margot was "inactive" in a sense, hanging around the camp as the men hunt and remaining in the automobile, she still has great control in the story. "Here, the woman is the one who, excluded from access to significant action, nevertheless has the power to destroy not only men's lives, but their self-constructs" (79).

## THE MANIPULATED WOMAN

### In His World

Women in Hemingway's life also existed who were controlled by his ways. Even those, or perhaps especially those, who once bore such a heavy presence in his life were subject to his domination. She may have lead him as a child, but Hemingway's mother did not even have her son present at her own funeral in 1951 (Buske 106). His lack of attendance was a statement. He did not allow her death to control his travels.

Even Stein, who gave him stiff guidance during his career beginnings, received the lash of his comments. Critic Linda Wagner-Martin explains that Hemingway often wrote poorly of Stein: "in his preface to Jimmy Charter's memoir, in the Joan Miro catalogue, in *For Whom the Bell Tolls*, in several unpublished pieces (most obviously in "the Autobiography of Alice B. Hemingway"), and in his dedication in the copy of *Green Hills of Africa* which he gave to Stein" Hemingway portrays Stein in a negative light (59). Even when they were close companions, Hemingway tried to stake some control in his relationship with Stein. Kennedy and Curnutt write that Hemingway wanted to get Stein to sleep with him, "perhaps in his mind to feminize her" (4). Likely, Hemingway was trying to prove he was man enough to direct Stein's sexuality. With both Stein and his mother, Hemingway seems to have been making every effort to control, in whatever manner he could, those who once dominated him.

### In His Work

Women under the control and manipulation of men are present in Hemingway's short fiction. In "Hills Like White Elephants," an American man is trying to convince his younger girlfriend to get an abortion. Paul Rankin describes the short story as such: "in an impressive feat of dialogue-driven narrative prose, Hemingway's unnamed American male protagonist dominates the meeker, weaker-sexed Jig . . . until, broken, she submits to his will and consents to aborting the child" (234). Roger Whitlow's take on the story is its being "Hemingway's most penetrating attack on man as the exploiter of woman" (qtd. in Bauer 129).

In a lecture on Hemingway, Gary Elliott explains that "everything the man says about the 'operation' is a lie, really. . . the man's affection for self is at the first place in his list of priorities." Indeed, the man describes the abortion as "really an awfully simple operation, Jig . . . It's not really an operation at all . . . I know you wouldn't mind it, Jig. It's really not anything. It's just to let the air in. . . They just let the air in and then it's all perfectly natural" (Hemingway 275). Joseph R. Urgo of Vanderbilt University agrees with Elliott's statement that the man's descriptions of the abortion are a lie when he states, "Whatever one's view on abortion, no medical operation can rightly be characterized as simple or natural" (36). The American man is using these reassurances to convince Jig to do what he wishes her to do.

Another method of manipulation the man uses is when he claims, seven times, within the story that he does not want to do it if she is unwilling, or if it is not what she wants. Gary Elliott describes the man's actions as "conniving and wimpish" in this section. The man claims to love the girl, though both Elliott and Hardy explain that the man does not really love this woman, at least not in the true definition of love, in a way that would satisfy her emotional or spiritual needs (10). The man says he cannot focus on her playful comment, such as the hills looking like white elephants, because he is too worried about their future. "I just can't think about it. You know how I get when I worry" (Hemingway 275). "Callous," as Dennis Organ describes him (11), the man works on Jig's hopes that things will be carefree as they used to, that he will be able to focus on her more, and that he will appreciate her for who she is in order to convince her of what she must do, what he is manipulating her towards doing.

In "The Snows of Kilimanjaro," the reader meets Harry and Helen, a couple struggling as Harry dies slowly of an infection complication. Harry's harsh comments towards his wife reveal his lack of love. Helen wants only to comfort Harry in his last moments, and he wants only to "quarrel" (Hemingway 53). What starts out as tense words from a dying man proves later to be the inner feelings of one who is using his wife for her money. When Helen claims, "Why, I loved you. That's not fair. I love you now. I'll always love you. Don't you love me?" Harry tells her bluntly, "No . . . I don't think so. I never have" (55). Eventually, Helen's pleading brings him to say, "I love you, really. You know I love you. I've never loved any one else the way I love you," after which he immediately internally calls these words "the familiar lie he made his bread and butter by" (58). He cannot keep his true feelings inside, though, and as he tells her, "You bitch . . . you rich bitch. That's poetry. I'm full of poetry now. Rot and poetry. Rotten poetry" (58). Later he thinks to himself about how he does not love this woman, "who had the most money of all, who had all the money there was," he only uses her for her wealth (60). He had loved others before Helen: "He had never quarreled much with this woman, while with the women that he loved he had quarreled so much they had finally, always, with the corrosion of the quarrelling, killed what they had together" (64). This statement, combined with those before it, prove that he is not with Helen because of her love, but because of her seemingly unlimited funds, funds that ironically brought him on this trip. Using her admiration of his writing, he gained access to these funds. With the women before her, he controlled those relationships too, in a way, by ruining them. "I don't like to leave anything. . . I don't like to leave things behind" he tells Helen (58). If this is truly his desire, he has succeeded by pushing away all who loved him.

THE WORTHLESS WOMAN

*In His World*

The final category of women in Hemingway's works and life are those who have little value to the men in their lives. Much speculation has been brought on by Hemingway's numerous marriages. After his love affair with Agnes, he married Elizabeth Hadley Richardson in 1921. During their courtship, Hadley would write to him, "I do love you very much. And I want to love you more. I mean to find more ways to show a thing so sweet and rare," to which Ernest Hemingway replied that he hoped to love her "a little while at least" (qtd. in Baker 77). On their honeymoon, Ernest took Hadley to meet some of his former girlfriends, remarking that he thought Hadley "would think more highly of him when she saw the girls he had rejected in her favor" (81). Instead, Hadley was hurt by Ernest's gross misunderstanding of woman's nature.

Eventually, Ernest Hemingway left Hadley for her friend, Pauline

Pfieffer in 1927. Again, in 1940, he left Pauline for her friend, Martha Gellhorn. His last marriage was to war correspondent Mary Welsh whom he met in 1944 ("Ernest Hemingway Biography"). His many marriages are reflective of Harry's in "Snows of Kilimanjaro." Possibly, arguments drove each marriage apart just as they did for Harry. More likely by the manner of his new relationships, marrying a woman close to his wife, Hemingway was just moving on to something new in his life. He treated his wives as many men do with a car, trading it in for a newer or different model as they grow tired of it.

*In His Work*

Women who are worthless to the men in the story are present in "Cat in the Rain" and "Indian Camp," both short stories from *In Our Time* published in 1925. Though the time period they were written proves that these women are not completely reflective of Hemingway's successive marriages, they are a reflection of the thinking he used when he married over and over again. In "Indian Camp," Dr. Adams proves his carelessness towards the woman giving birth in many ways. He calls her "lady" even though he treats her more like he would an animal. Also, he has come to this birth completely ill prepared. When Nick asks if Dr. Adams can give the woman something to keep her from screaming, his father replies, "No. I haven't any anæsthetic" (Hemingway 92). Why would the doctor come to do his job without the appropriate items that may be necessary if a complicated birth arose? Also, Dr. Adams refers to the woman's screams of pain as "not important. I don't hear them because they are not important" when it is obvious they are important to several other people in the room, including Nick, who is set ill at ease by them, and the Indian woman's husband, who kills himself because of them (92). Even a young Indian who is watching the action feels no sympathy for the woman, as he laughs when George calls her a foul name (93).

After the surgery, Dr. Adams considers himself quite the success for having performed the Cæsarian with "a jack-knife and sewing it up with nine-foot, tapered gut leaders," when he should be ashamed that it came to that because of his poor preparation (Hemingway 94). The woman is not a person to him, but a chance to show off his innovation. He feels "exalted and talkative as football players are in the dressing room after a game" (94). When he finally notices that the woman's husband has killed himself over the matter, he cannot assume that it happened because of the man's feelings for the woman, since Dr. Adams has none for her, but simply because men are "usually the worst sufferers in these little affairs" (94). Not only does this comment give too much credit to men, it also reduces the importance of one of woman's greatest accomplishments, the ability to withstand the pains in order to give birth to a child, to make new life for this world. Dr. Adams cannot see the event as such because he is completely unaware of the woman throughout the experience. He comes unprepared, ignores her screams, and discounts her pains and efforts throughout the birth. Dr. Adams does not believe this woman, or her exertion that day, are of any value.

Likewise, the husband in "Cat in the Rain" does not have any interest in his wife. The American wife views something outside of her foreign hotel that she desires: "Outside right under their window a cat was crouched under one of the dripping green tables. The cat was trying to make herself so compact that she would not be dripped on" (Hemingway 167). Many critics speculate the meaning behind the woman's wanting this cat. Hildy Coleman believes the cat is "a metaphorical child" her husband will not let her have (68-69). Peter Griffin feels the cat symbolizes the desire for physical arousal that the woman cannot get from her husband who is "dry, desiccated, and unable or unwilling to act" (102).

Whatever the symbolism, the point remains that the wife wants the cat, and her husband, George, has absolutely no interest in helping her meet this desire. When the wife says she is going to go down and "get that kitty," her husband blandly offers, "I'll do it" (Hemingway 167). Hemingway cleverly keeps the man in the same position, doing the same action, for the entire story, though, to show readers that such an offer in not made with true feeling. The man "only lies in bed, propped up on pillows, and reads," Griffin explains (101). Warren Bennett of the University of Regina notes, the husband "doesn't even look up from his book. His activity throughout the story is limited to 'putting the book down' (93), 'resting his eyes' (93), and, on one occasion, 'shift[ing] his position in the bed' (93)" (31). When the wife begins to leave the room, Hemingway writes that "the husband went on reading, lying propped up with the two pillows at the foot of the bed 'Don't get wet,' he said" (167-68). Bennett takes off on the husband's comment:

> He does not have enough commitment to his wife to care that she is leaving the room with neither umbrella nor rainwear to go out in the rain. Later, when she returns without the cat, George asks, without looking up from his book, "Did you get the cat?" (93). If he were seriously interested, he would look up and see that she doesn't have a cat. And since he does not look up, he has no concern that his wife might be wet. (31)

When she does not get the cat she desired, the wife begins to make a list of things she wants:

> I want to pull my hair back tight and smooth and make a big knot at the back that I can feel. . . I want to have a kitty to sit on my lap and purr when I stroke her . . . and I want to eat at a table with my own silver and I want candles. And I want it to be spring and I want to brush my hair out in front of a mirror and I want a kitty and I want some new clothes. (Hemingway 169-70)

Her desires all have a consistent theme. First of all, she wants affection. She assumes that having a cat will give her a companion who both receives her love and gives her affirmation, as seen in her wanting the kitty to sit with her and make purring sounds while she loves on it. Secondly, she wants to be viewed as very womanly, perhaps thinking that having long hair, fine dinners, and new clothes will spark an interest in her from her listless husband.

### IN THE END

Hemingway's title has a double meaning. Bennett explains the woman in the story is reacting to "George's lack of character, his indifference, and his rejection of her rightful place in the relationship. The effect is a sense of homelessness, similar to the condition of a homeless cat in the rain" (31). Not only does the wife desire the cat she saw in the rain, she is the symbolic cat in the rain.

Though much has been made in efforts to say that Hemingway's stories are direct biographical instants from his life, this idea is too much of a stretch.  For example, Jeffrey Meyers tries to connect "Cat in the Rain" with "the disintegration of [Ernest's] marriage to Hadley" and connects the woman in the story with the pregnant Mrs. Hemingway (144).  Bennett, however, spends much of his time in "The Poor Kitty and the Padrone and the Tortoise-shell Cat in 'Cat in the Rain'" in refuting this statement.  When a true critical reader looks into timing issues, Hemingway's letters, and keys in the story, he could see that this story does not connect to Hadley's pregnancy (26-35).  Still, connections to Hemingway's life are abundant in his fiction.  Hemingway's relationships to women in particular, though not always represented in their entirely, are reflected in his short stories.  In his life, women were controlling of, controlled by, and of little value to him, and women of the same sort appear in several of his tales.  A writer cannot be good at his craft without letting his own experiences and feelings show up in his work, and Hemingway is considered one of the best.  His desire to be true in his writing led him to connect his fiction with his life, and his life with his fiction, until the two nearly become blurred into one.  Hemingway's works and his life are both subject of much critical discovery and will be for years to come.

BIBLIOGRAPHY

Adair, William.  "A Source for Hemingway's 'Indian Camp.'"  *Studies in Short Fiction* 28.1 (1991): 93-95.  Print.

Baker, Carlos.  "The Country and the Town."  *Ernest Hemingway: A Life Story*.  New York: Charles Scribner's Sons, 1969. 1-8.  Print.

---.  "Hadley."  *Ernest Hemingway: A Life Story*.  New York: Charles Scribner's Sons, 1969. 75-83.  Print.

---.  "Juvenila."  *Ernest Hemingway: A Life Story*.  New York: Charles Scribner's Sons, 1969.  17-29.  Print.

---.  "Milano."  *Ernest Hemingway: A Life Story*.  New York: Charles Scribner's Sons, 1969.  46-56.  Print.

---. "A Search for the Man as He Really Was." *The New York Times on the Web.* n.p. 26 July 1964. Web. 12 April 2006.

---. "Soldier's Home." *Ernest Hemingway: A Life Story.* New York: Charles Scribner's Sons, 1969. 56-64. Print.

Bauer, Margaret D. "Forget the Legend and Read the Work: Teaching Two Stories by Ernest Hemingway." *College Literature* 30.3 (2003): 124-37. Print.

Bennett, Warren. "The Poor Kitty and the Padrone and the Tortoise shell Cat in 'Cat in the Rain.'" *The Hemingway Review* 8.1 (1988): 26-36. Print.

Buske, Morris. "The Soldier's Home Again." *The Hemingway Review* 15.2 (1996): 104-07. Print.

Coleman, Hildy. "'Cat' and 'Hills': Two Hemingway Fairy Tales." *The Hemingway Review* 12.1 (1992): 67-72. Print.

Elliott, Gary. "Hemingway's 'Hills Like White Elephants.'" *Explicator* 35.4 (1977): 22-23. Print.

---. "Hemingway's 'The Light of the World.'" *Explicator* 40.1 (1981): 48-49. Print.

---. Lecture. Harding University, Arkansas. 4 Apr. 2006.

---. "Ernest Hemingway Biography." *The Hemingway Resource Center. Lostgeneration.com.* n.p. n.d. Web. 17 Jan. 2012.

---. "Ernest Hemingway Biography and Notes." *Biblio.com.* n.p. n.d. Web. 17 Jan. 2012.

Felty, Darren. "Spatial Confinement in Hemingway's 'Cat in the Rain.'" *Studies in Short Fiction* 34.3 (1997): 363-69. Print.

Fulkerson, Richard. "The Biographical Fallacy and 'The Doctor and the Doctor's Wife.'" *Studies in Short Fiction* 16 (61-65). Print.

Griffin, Peter. "A Foul Mood, a Dirty Joke: Hemingway's 'Cat in the Rain.'" *The Hemingway Review* 20.2 (2001): 99-102. Print.

Hardy, Donald E. "Presupposition and the Coconspirator." *Style* 26.1 (1992): 1-11. Print.

Hemingway, Ernest. "Cat in the Rain." *The Short Stories*. New York: Scribner, 1995. 165-70. Print.

---. "Hills Like White Elephants." *The Short Stories*. New York: Scribner, 1995. 273-78. Print.

---. "Indian Camp." *The Short Stories*. New York: Scribner, 1995. 89-96. Print.

---. Introduction. *The Short Stories*. New York: Scribner, 1995. Print.

---. "The Short Happy Life of Francis Macomber." *The Short Stories*. New York: Scribner, 1995. 3-37. Print.

---. "Soldier's Home." *The Short Stories*. New York: Scribner, 1995. 143-54. Print

---. "Snows of Kilimanjaro." *The Short Stories*. New York: Scribner, 1995. 52-77. Print.

---. Nobel Prize Speech. Nobel Banquet, Stockholm. 10 Dec. 1954.

Kennedy, Gerald J., and Kirk Curnutt. "Out of the Picture: Mrs. Krebs, Mother Stein, and 'Soldier's Home.'" *The Hemingway Review* 12.1 (1992): 1-11. Print.

Madison, Robert D. "Hemingway and Selous: A Source for 'Snows'?" *The Hemingway Review* 8.1 (1988): 62-63. Print.

Monteiro, George. "Waifs and Driftwood – A Melvillean Theme in Hemingway's 'The Doctor and the Doctor's Wife.'" *Studies in Short Fiction* 27.1 (1990): 99-100. Print.

Organ, Dennis. "Hemingway's 'Hills Like White Elephants.'" *Explicator* 31.4 (1979): 11. Print.

Rankin, Paul. "Hemingway's 'Hills Like White Elephants.'" *Explicator* 63.4 (2005): 234-37. Print.

Urgo, Joseph R. "Hemingway's 'Hills Like White Elephants.'" *Explicator* 46.3 (1988): 35-37. Print.

Wagner-Martin, Linda. "A Note on Henri Rousseau and Hemingway's 'The Snows of Kilimanjaro.'" *The Hemingway Review* 11.1 (1991): 58-59. Print.

Wolter, Jürgen C. "Caesareans in 'Indian Camp.'" *The Hemingway Review* 13.1 (1993): 92-94. Print.

Kelly Young is an instructor in the Interior Design Department at O'More College of Design. She is NCIDQ certified and a registered Interior Designer at City Tile and Floor Covering in Murfreesboro, Tennessee. Young received a Bachelor of Science in Human Environmental Sciences at the University of Tennessee, Martin.

# FIRE PREVENTATIVE
## AND SO MUCH MORE—
### A REGISTERED INTERIOR DESIGNER

### KELLY YOUNG
*Instructor, Interior Design*

CAN YOU IMAGINE what you'd do if you were caught in a fire? After the shock and panic, your adrenaline would probably kick in, and you'd race toward the nearest exit. Once you were safe, you'd start to wonder how the fire started, or what you could have done to prevent it.

When a home or building is struck by a fire, there are specific questions that need to be answered: were signs placed in a manner that directed occupants to the exit; how far did occupants have to travel to safely exit the building; and, if necessary, could the occupants climb out a window? Additionally, were the hallway and door openings wide enough for the number of occupants (including disabled occupants), and were the stairwells designed to remain intact longer so more occupants could escape to safety?

Who is responsible for making sure building occupants were able to make it to safety? Numerous parties were involved in construction, such as the architect and builder, but what if the fire generated from the window treatments? The window treatments were not up to building code, but the owner hired a decorating professional to assist in the selection.

Here in lies the problem: a "decorator" was hired, not a NCIDQ certified or licensed and registered interior designer.

What is the difference?

The NCIDQ (National Council of Interior Design Qualifications) certified interior designers have been tested about not only color and design theory, but building codes, space planning, contract administration, ADA requirement, historical periods, etc. After a designer passes the NCIDQ exam, he or she goes on to apply for state registration to use the title of Licensed or Registered interior designer. Once approved by the state this means a person is qualified by education, experience, and examination and meets all the requirements set forth by the Department of Commerce.

There is a difference between the title of "Licensed and Registered interior designer" and "interior designer" depending on the state you reside in. Currently twenty five states have practice acts protecting the title of "interior designer" as one who is qualified. For those states that do not one must look for Licensed and Registered interior designer. (This title is protected by a title act.)

There is a group called the IDPC (Interior Design Protection Council) who is fighting practice act regulation. If the IDPC feels that adamant about being considered equal in the world of interior design, then perhaps they should encourage those who are decorators to become NCIDQ certified and registered with their state. It will require education, work experience, and certification, but will cause these individuals to be qualified for so much more than decorating.

On the opposing side is the Interior Design Coalition. This organization is lobbying for practice acts and advancement of the interior design profession. They want to ensure that the extra work and education put into an interior design career is distinguished from the term "decorator," which any person can profess.

If you want a worthy cause to donate to, research ASID (American Society of Interior Designer) or IIDA (International Interior Design Association). Both of these organizations support NCIDQ and registered interior designers. They will assist you in finding a designer who fits your needs.

When building or remodeling, keep in mind the importance of being fire preventative. Hire an interior designer that is NCIDQ certified or a registered interior designer.

# A Special Thanks

O'MORE PUBLISHING would like to thank those instructors, professors, and students who took the time to write about what is important to them in their field for this publication. We, and the rest of O'More College of Design, are also grateful to our artist in residence from this school year: Lori Bumgarner. Her contributions to the school have not gone unnoticed or unappreciated.

We would also like to thank those whose design work enhances this book: book designer Courtney Allen (student, Visual Communications); book designer and illustrator Sarah Keaggy (student, Visual Communications); photographer Malerie Serley (student, Visual Communications); journalist Ashley Balding (student, Fashion Design); and art director and designer Whitnee Webb.

CPSIA information can be obtained at www.ICGtesting.com
Printed in the USA
LVOW090048020512

279834LV00001B/9/P